For the Love of
KNITTING

A Celebration of the Knitter's Art

Kari Cornell, Editor

With writings, artwork, and photographs from
Melanie Falick, Elizabeth Zimmermann, Meg Swansen,
Pam Allen, Perri Klass, Jamaica Kincaid, Susan Gordon Lydon,
Lela Nargi, Teva Durham, Chris Hartlove, Sandy Nicholson, Brian Céré,
Debbie New, Solveig Hisdal, and more.

Voyageur Press

Edited by Kari Cornell
Designed by Maria Friedrich
Printed in China

04 05 06 07 08 5 4 3 2 1

Library of Congress Cataloging-in-Publication Data

For the love of knitting : a celebration of the knitter's art / Kari Cornell, editor ; with writings, artwork, and photographs from Melanie Falick ... [et al.].
    p. cm.
  ISBN 0-89658-045-8 (hardcover)
  1. Knitting. I. Cornell, Kari A. II. Falick, Melanie.
  TT820.F67 2004
  746.43'2—dc22
                    2004005041

Published by Voyageur Press, Inc.
123 North Second Street, P.O. Box 338
Stillwater, MN 55082 U.S.A.
651-430-2210, fax 651-430-2211
books@voyageurpress.com
www.voyageurpress.com

Educators, fundraisers, premium and gift buyers, publicists, and marketing managers: Looking for creative products and new sales ideas? Voyageur Press books are available at special discounts when purchased in quantities, and special editions can be created to your specifications. For details contact the marketing department at 800-888-9653.

On the front cover: Top and bottom left photographs © Sandy Nicholson Photography; Bottom middle and right © Chris Hartlove.

On the back cover: Top left (Boys knitting) photograph by St. Paul Dispatch-Pioneer Press, courtesy of the Minnesota Historical Society; Bottom left (Ladies knitting and spinning) photograph © Chris Hartlove.

On the frontispiece: In this charming painting from the eighteenth century, a mother knits while her daughter looks on.

On the title page: Tiffany Quilt, 1997, was designed by Debbie New for her book Unexpected Knitting. The colorful piece is loosely knit in mohair and sandwiched between two layers of tulle. (Photograph © Brian Céré of Dumont Group Photography, Kitchener, Ont.)

Inset on the title page: Women gather in Saint Paul, Minnesota to learn to knit in a class offered by the Works Progress Administration, circa 1938. (Photograph courtesy of the Minnesota Historical Society)

On the facing page: A sampling of knitting swatches illustrates the wide range of color and stitch pattern variations available to the knitter. (Photograph © Chris Hartlove)

On the contents page: Skeins of yarn in rich, vibrant tones stack the shelves of a local yarn shop. (Photograph © Chris Hartlove)

Permissions

"Learning to Knit" from *Knitting Around* by Elizabeth Zimmerman. Copyright © 1989 by Elizabeth Zimmermann. Used by permission of Schoolhouse Press.

"So Begins a Fetish" from *Knitting Lessons: Tales from the Knitting Path* by Lela Nargi. Copyright © 2003 by Lela Nargi. Used by permission of Penguin Group USA, Inc.

"Knitting" from *Talk Stories* by Jamaica Kincaid. Copyright © 2001 by Jamaica Kincaid. Reprinted by permission of Farrar, Straus and Giroux, LLC.

"A Bunch of Little Old Ladies" from *Knit Lit: Sweaters and Their Stories . . . And Other Writing about Knitting*, edited by Linda Roghaar and Molly Wolf. Copyright © 2002 by Kay Dorn. Used by permission of the author.

"Two Sweaters for My Father" by Perri Klass was first published as a shorter column in the winter 2002 issue of *Knitter's* magazine. Used by permission of the author.

"Knit Gallery: The Search for a Proper Place among the Arts" by Teva Durham was first published as a shorter Ravelings column in the fall 2003 issue of *Interweave Knits* magazine. Used by permission of the author.

"Dreaming of Dragons" from *The Knitting Sutra: Craft as a Spiritual Practice* by Susan Gordon Lydon. Copyright © 1997 by Susan Gordon Lydon. Reprinted by permission of HarperCollins Publishers Inc.

"When Knitting Was a Manly Art" by Clinton W. Trowbridge was first published in the *Christian Science Monitor*. Used by permission of the author.

ACKNOWLEDGMENTS

This book would not have been possible without the help of many dedicated people. I'd like to express my gratitude to all those who contributed their stories, photographs, artwork, time, and talent to the project: J. C. Allen & Sons, Inc., Pam Allen, Carol Anderson, Nancy Bush, Brian Céré, Lily Chin, Betty Christiansen, Katharine Cobey, Kay Dorn, Kaffe Fassett, Alvaro Gonzales, Chris Hartlove, Solveig Hisdal, Suzyn Jackson, Jamaica Kincaid, Perri Klass, Linda Ligon, Susan Gordon Lydon, Lela Nargi, Debbie New, Sandy Nicholson, Karen Searle, Clinton W. Trowbridge, Amy Votava, and Lois S. Young.

I owe a special thank you to Margret Aldrich, Sigrid Arnott, Naomi Dagen Bloom, Michael Dregni, Teva Durham, Melanie Falick, Maria Friedrich, Denyse Specktor, and Meg Swansen, who offered new ideas, inspiration, and encouragement throughout the process. Last but by no means least, I'd like to thank my husband, Brian, for his never-ending support, and my friends from knitting club for providing knitting lessons and friendship.

CONTENTS

J. & P. COATS · CLARK'S **O.N.T.**   SWEATERS   BOOK No. 504   **25¢**

SWEATERS
For the Family

CHADWICK'S **RED** HEART YARNS

FOR THE LOVE OF KNITTING

In the past, knitting has brought to mind the stereotypical image of a gray-haired grandmother, whiling away the hours on a Sunday afternoon in her favorite rocking chair with her latest knitting project on her lap. To some extent, especially among those who do not knit, this image remains intact. But if you look around you, whether you're on the bus, subway, or train; in a waiting room; or in the stands at a little league baseball game, you'll begin to notice that knitting isn't just for grandmothers anymore. Teachers in private Waldorf schools teach knitting to first-graders to improve their concentration and motor skills. Freshman in colleges across the country gather in dorm rooms and coffee shops to knit quick hats on big needles and exchange a few morsels of juicy gossip. Those of all ages who learned to knit once upon a time as children are revisiting the skill, this time sticking with it.

Shortly after this book was underway, my husband and I were walking down a city street in Seattle when we saw a sight that defied all knitting stereotypes. There, leaning on a bus shelter was a very hip young man, dressed in black, knitting to pass the time as he waited for the bus. I didn't want to stare, but I couldn't help smiling as I glanced back over my shoulder a few times at this most welcome scene. Since then, I've encountered more people knitting in public than I can count, and each sighting has reinforced the fact that knitting is alive and well in America.

When the craft first took hold long ago, it wasn't so unusual to see a man knitting in public. Although exactly when people first began to knit and where the craft originated is unclear, fishermen and shepherds are believed to have been the first knitters, stitching away as they waited to pull in their nets or move their flock. Women would spin the wool from home while they cared for the children.

The earliest examples of knitting have long since disintegrated, so it is difficult to date the craft. The oldest knit-like fragments still in existence are from the third century A.D. and were unearthed in the Middle East. Upon close examination, however, these fabrics were found to be examples of nålbinding, a technique that produces a cloth similar to knitting, but with a twisted stitch. The oldest knitted items in existence—blue and white cotton socks—were found in Egypt and are believed to date from between 1200 and 1500 A.D. These early examples appear to have been worked in the round, on either four or five needles, and historians speculate that purling was developed later.

Knitting is believed to have spread from the Middle East to Spain via Moorish invaders during the Middle Ages. By the fourteenth century, the craft had clearly taken its

The Knitting Grandmother
Although she's not seated in a rocking chair, this grandmotherly type pictured on the back cover of a vintage Red Heart pattern book from 1953 exemplifies the old knitting stereotype.

place among the list of tasks suitable for women, as Italian and German artists had begun to depict the Virgin Mary holding needles and yarn in their paintings.

Meanwhile, upper-class Europeans had begun to favor the comfort and versatility of stockings knit from wool and silk, and it wasn't long before the poor were knitting stockings, gloves, caps, and shirts as a way to make money. During the fifteenth and sixteenth centuries, knitting guilds had sprung up in Europe, each specializing in the production of a particular item. Most if not all guild members were men. Perhaps the best-known knitting guild was the Guild of St. Fiacra, a group based in Paris in the early 1500s that only knitted caps.

By the seventeenth century, knitting had spread north into Scandinavia and east into Russia. When European immigrants settled on American soil, they introduced knitting to the native peoples. Several countries and regions developed unique stitch and color patterns, and those patterns spread to other areas along trade routes. The regions in which specific traditional patterns originally developed have long been known for their unique contribution to the world of knitting. Norwegian knitters create intricately patterned two-color Setesdal sweaters while the Swedes stitch beautiful multicolored Bohus sweaters. Colorwork also defines the Fair Isle knitting tradition on the remote island off the northern coast of Scotland. The handicraft of Fair Isle knitters shares many similarities with colorwork from Spain, leading historians to believe that the Spaniards may have introduced their technique to the islanders when one of their ships was marooned on the island's coast. Knitters in fishing villages throughout the British Isles, particularly in Devon and Cornwall, make single-colored sweaters known as ganseys in a hardy wool, richly textured with cables, ribs, and bobbles. Each fishing village claims its own design.

Prior to the Industrial Revolution in the eighteenth century, every young girl learned to knit and sew, as many families made their own clothes. In parts of England, knitters would gather around the warmth of the fireplace at a neighbor's home, talking and telling stories as they knit through the afternoon. During times of war or economic hardship, women, men, and children would join forces to knit warm clothes or blankets for soldiers or the poor and underprivileged. But as knitting mills began to mass produce socks, sweaters, mittens, caps, and other knit goods at a very low cost, handknitting became more of a hobby than a necessity.

Throughout most of history, knitting has been considered women's work, a task that could easily be done while caring for children. As women earned the right to vote and slowly began to enter the workforce, knitting became a symbol of the dreary existence they had worked so hard to overcome. In the 1960s and 1970s, when the women's liberation movement was at its peak, many women stopped knitting as a way of protesting the years of inequality they had endured.

Since the early 1990s, however, knitting has experienced a renaissance. Those new to knitting and many returning knitters are taking needles and yarn in hand and

The First Knitters
It makes sense that shepherds would have been among the first knitters, with a steady supply of wool and time throughout the day to knit row after row. (Photograph © J. C. Allen & Sons, Inc.)

taking to heart the empowering words of Elizabeth Zimmermann, Barbara G. Walker, and Debbie New, whose books encourage knitters to take control of their craft instead of blindly following each and every pattern. Knitting's renewed popularity has grown with the introduction of new novelty yarns and inspiration from Kaffe Fasset and Annabel Fox, whose work with color has revolutionized everyday patterns.

What is knitting's appeal? Many claim it is the tactile nature of knitting, the soft, comforting feeling of the yarn slipping through their fingers only seconds before assuming its place in a line-up of loops on their needles. Others swear by the meditative quality of knitting, the repetitive motion that quickly erases the day's tension and worries. Like a good book, a knitting project has the ability to carry the knitter into a different world. And, for those who belong to knitting clubs, the craft provides the perfect excuse for getting together with friends for a couple of hours of good conversation and more than a few laughs. Overachievers glom on to knitting as a way to multitask—now they can actually accomplish something while watching TV in the evenings. Whatever its appeal is to you, knitting is here to stay.

The wide variety of essays and stories contained within the pages of this anthology celebrate the appeal and love of this age-old art. The funny, heartwarming, and sometimes sad tales of Jamaica Kincaid, Elizabeth Zimmermann, Perri Klass, Pam Allen, Naomi Dagen Bloom, Susan Gordon Lydon, Melanie Falick, Meg Swansen, Lela Nargi, Teva Durham, Lily M. Chin, Clinton W. Trowbridge, and Denyse Specktor touch on all aspects of knitting, from shearing the sheep to giving the finely knitted hat, sweater, or socks as a gift. The work of many talented artists and photographers, including Chris Hartlove, Sandy Nicholson, Brian Céré, Debbie New, Solveig Hisdal, Alvaro J. Gonzalez, Jean Francois Millet, and Jozef Israels, illustrate the text.

I hope you enjoy this tribute to knitting as much as I've enjoyed assembling it, one knit-stitch at a time.

Spin, Spin!
Women were spinners before they were knitters. Röslein, the subject of this quirky German postcard, seems none-too-pleased with the task at hand.

Dutch Maiden
A young Dutch maiden knits contently by the sea in this vintage, hand-colored postcard.

W.T. Benda

You can help
AMERICAN RED CROSS

You Can Help

The American Red Cross organized troops of knitters on the homefront, providing them with very specific patterns for items the young soldiers badly needed and ensuring that shipments of completed knitwear reached the frontlines in a timely manner. Posters, such as this reproduction by W. T. Benda, called knitters to action.

A Few Stitches between Chores
The portable nature of a small knitted project made it easy for 1930s housewives to fill time between chores by knitting a few rows. This image by Ralph Pallen Coleman graced the cover of the September 1935 issue of Home Arts *magazine.*

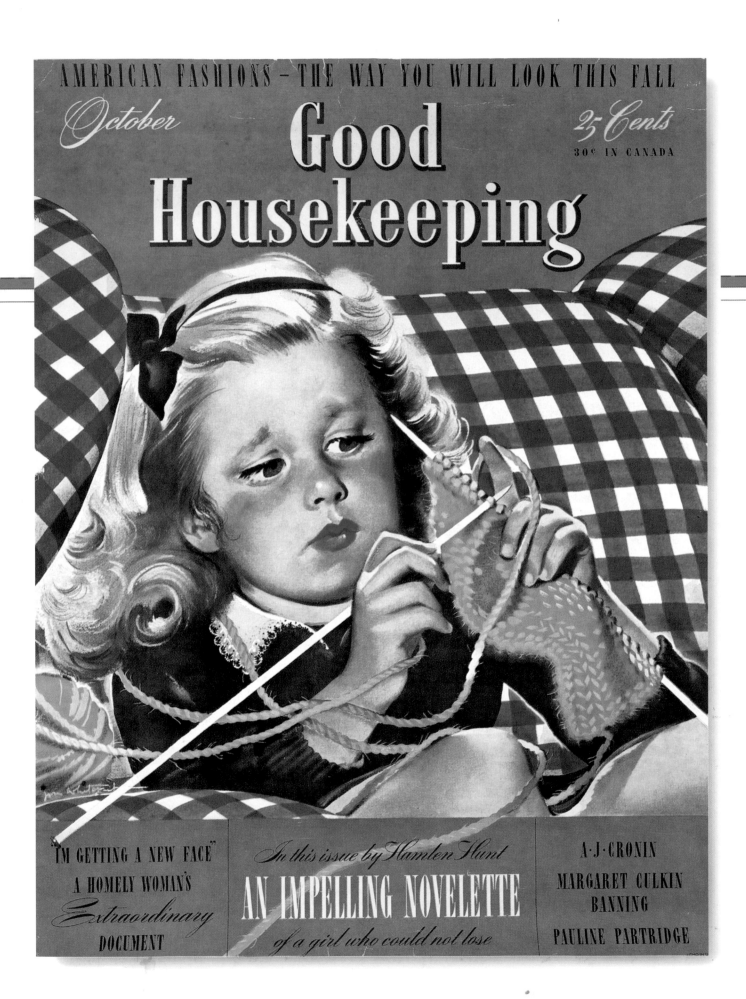

CHAPTER 1

KNITTING THE FIRST STITCH

"TAKE A NEEDLE IN EACH HAND," SHE SAID, "AND PUT THE RIGHTHAND NEEDLE INTO THE FIRST STITCH ON THE LEFTHAND NEEDLE. NOW PICK UP THE WOOL WITH YOUR RIGHT HAND, AND LOOP IT ROUND THE RIGHTHAND NEEDLE, FROM BACK TO FRONT. THEN HOICK IT THROUGH THE OTHER STITCH, THE ONE ON THE LEFTHAND NEEDLE, SLIPPING THIS STITCH OFF."

"SEE?" SHE SAID. "ONE STITCH KNITTED! LET'S DO IT AGAIN."

–Elizabeth Zimmerman, Knitting Around, 1989

All knitters, no matter how advanced they may be today, were once beginners. Some may have learned to knit as children, so the memories of that first clumsy stitch faded long ago. But for those who first picked up a pair of knitting needles later in life, it is likely that the experience is still imprinted vividly in their minds. They may remember the strange feeling of holding the needles in their hands, the intensity with which they focused on looping the yarn the correct way around the working needle, the stitch or cast-on technique that they had to learn and relearn. The stories collected in this chapter are all about learning to knit, but as you may expect, the experiences are as varied and unique as the knitters themselves.

Good Housekeeping Learns to Knit
The beginning knitter on this 1950s Good Housekeeping cover furrows her brow with concentration as she attempts to knit her first project.

Handmade Knitting Needles
A pottery mug filled with colorful, handmade knitting needles entices new knitters to try the craft. (Photograph © Chris Hartlove)

NEW LUX KNITTING BOOK

1951 EDITION

76 designs for the whole family

50¢

Learning to Knit

By Elizabeth Zimmermann

British-born master knitter Elizabeth Zimmermann (1910–1999) has long been a touchstone for those who are picking up needles for the first time. Zimmermann revolutionized knitting when she founded Schoolhouse Press in 1959, a company dedicated to providing circular needles, natural wool, and a commonsense knitting philosophy to American knitters. Author of Knitting Without Tears, Knitting Around, Elizabeth Zimmermann's Knitter's Almanac, and Elizabeth Zimmermann's Knitter's Workshop, four books that remain all-time favorites among knitters today, Elizabeth also wrote countless articles that appeared in magazines such as Knitter's and Threads. She also hosted a learn-to-knit program on public television and began a summer knitting camp in Wisconsin, which her daughter, Meg Swansen, continues to organize to this day.

Zimmermann's infectious sense of humor and her straightforward, no-nonsense approach to knitting has earned her a special place in the hearts of all those fortunate enough to discover her philosophy. This essay about learning to knit first appeared in Knitting Around, a book of patterns and digressions about Zimmermann's life published by Schoolhouse Press in 1989.

One of my earliest memories has always been of a day when I pestered my mother to teach me how to knit. The female half of my mother's family knitted uninterruptably, and they rather scorned the females of my father's family who knitted exclusively mats and potholders.

"Well," said my mother, "If you're good all day today, I'll teach you tomorrow."

A woman of her word she was, so I was GOOD . . . all day. The next day, Mummy was sitting in the dining-room, knitting around. I can see that sweater (jersey to us, of course) to this day. It was bright green, in stocking-stitch, on four needles (no circulars in those days), and destined for me myself. So I perched on her lap and she put her knitting in front of me.

"Take a needle in each hand," she said, "and put the righthand needle into the first stitch on the lefthand needle. Now pick up the wool with your right hand, and loop it round the righthand needle, from back to front. Then hoick it through the other stitch, the one on the lefthand needle, slipping this stitch off."

This was repeated several times, to the poetic remark of "slip, over, under, off."

"See?" she said. "One stitch knitted! Let's do it again." So we did. And then a third time.

"That's enough for today," she said.

Such excitement. She must have taught me to purl sometime too, but of this I have no recollection except that it was a bit awkward to achieve.

I took that sweater with me and wore it when we all went for that summer in Polzeath; all except my father, who was in a battleship in the North Sea. When Auntie Pete came to visit us there, I proudly showed her my knitting. She extin-

Like Mother, Like Daughter
On the cover of this vintage pattern book, published by Lux in 1951, a mother teaches her daughter how to knit step by step. For a mere fifty cents, the book provided seventy-six easy-to-follow patterns to create knitwear for the whole family.

guished my pride immediately by showing me *her* knitting: four of the skinniest little double-pointed needles, deeply involved in a circular piece of knitting about three inches long. It was to be a sock.

"Show me!"

So she did. Off I went, on to the cliffs, to knit, and had the time of my life. I soon discovered that I was working a bit loosely, so tightened up a bit, especially when moving from one needle to the next.

Later that day, Auntie Pete demanded her knitting back, so as to be able to get on with it herself, and gently commented on its looseness where one needle had joined another. I was cut to the quick, but said nothing, possibly having instinctively realized My Life Was Starting. When she ripped my few rows, my little heart almost broke. But I'd learned HOW TO KNIT, and have never stopped since.

The Greenwood family consisted of a bunch of excellent knitters. My Auntie Carol even contributed sweater designs to *Walson's Magazine*, and of course they all "threw their wool" with the right hand, which I did too.

* * *

One morning, there, in front of the gas-stove sat the Swiss Governess Hélene, a long blue stocking for the baby-sister hanging from four regular knitting needles—but what was *that*? The stocking was slowly growing, but the hands weren't knitting; the right hand hooked the stitches through all right, but around the *left* forefinger was looped the wool itself.

"Montrez moi," I said. And she did. I was fascinated, and I immediately set to practising this new, and obviously more efficient way of knitting.

Before long, Miss Barrett made her entrance, poised for the morning's lessons.

She took one look at me and said, "What are you doing?"

I said, "Knitting, Miss Barrett."

"KNITTING!" she said. "Don't you know that's the GERMAN WAY TO KNIT? I absolutely forbid you to knit that way. *Real* knitting is Slip, Over, Under, Off."

"Yes, Miss Barrett," and I took the wool in the Other Hand and continued to knit in the idiom of my ancestors. Miss Barrett lasted about six weeks (the Kentish climate was too much for her), but Hélene stayed on for years, taught us French, and I contacted her some years later in Lausanne. To this day, I continue to knit with the wool over the left forefinger, but hold a strand of wool in either hand for all colour-pattern knitting.

Tension Tamer
Winding the working yarn around her index finger to provide just enough tension, a knitter stitches a textural bouclé yarn into a luxurious scarf. (Photograph © David P. Austin)

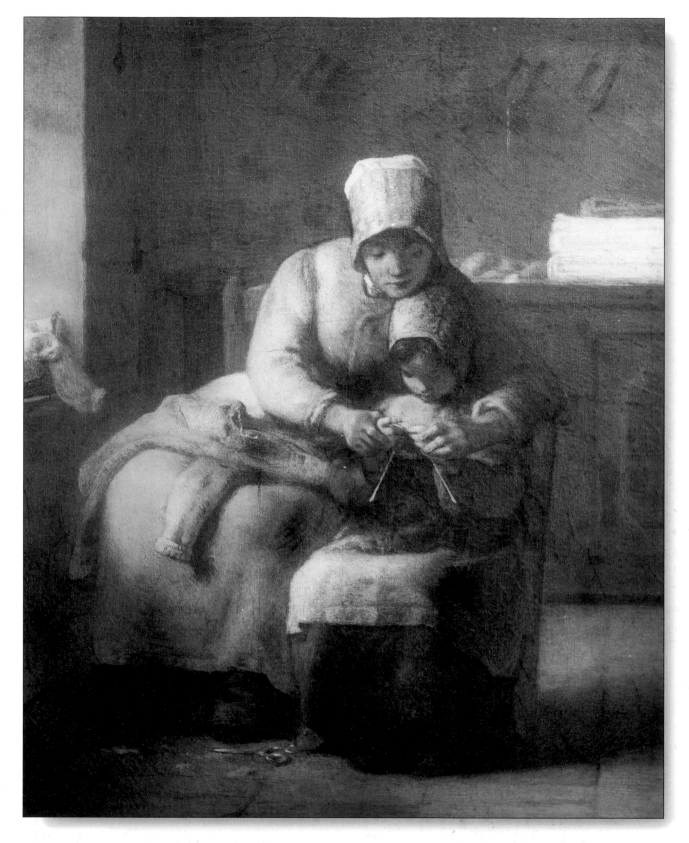

"The Knitting Lesson"
With great care and gentleness, a mother guides her daughter's hands through the motions of knitting a stocking in this late-nineteenth-century painting by French artist Jean-François Millet. (Print courtesy of the Library of Congress)

Her Hands

By Betty Christiansen

Most knitters are so passionate about their craft that they can't imagine life without it. They are forever indebted to the mother, grandmother, or friend who taught them to knit. In "Her Hands," family friend Oleeta is the knitter who passed her gift on to author Betty Christiansen.

Betty is a knitter, writer, and editor living in Brownsville, Minnesota, with her husband, Andrew Miles. She has an MFA in creative nonfiction writing from Sarah Lawrence College. Her work has been published in Interweave Knits, Vogue Knitting, Family Circle Easy Knitting, Creative Nonfiction, and KnitLit (too): Stories from Sheep to Shawl . . . and More Writing About Knitting.

The summer I was nine, I learned to knit. It was 1978, the year the grandmother who might have taught me died, the year I was finally old enough to join 4-H, the year I got glasses, the year the tiny country schools around my tiny Wisconsin town closed, consolidating into mine. Except for 4-H, it was a pretty bad year.

At nine, I stopped being a little girl and started becoming something else. My hair, once soft and honey blond, became the color of dishwater and hung in my eyes. I still wore homemade outfits in wild polyester prints; my classmates wore jeans. And since I'd been caught squinting at the chalkboard, square plastic frames with heavy lenses had become a permanent fixture on my face. My friends found new friends among the "country kids," and they formed a secret club in a juniper grove in the schoolyard, to which I was *not* admitted. "Learn to be your own best friend," my mother told me, gently, when I came home crying. Later, in an unrelated move, she scavenged yarn and needles from projects my grandmother never completed and sent me to Oleeta's.

Oleeta was a Danish woman who lived in a small farmhouse like ours in the same Danish community we did. She and her husband were older than my parents, but not yet my grandparents' age, and when we were growing up, they were a constant in our lives, supplying last-minute babysitting, lots of encouragement, and plenty of love.

Oleeta, I remember, was soft in every way. Her eyes were soft, her laugh lines deep and ever-present—she was always smiling. Her hair was soft, a light gray. Her voice was like music, like a cardinal's song. Only her hands weren't soft, weathered instead from gardening, peeling apples, picking berries. Her kitchen smelled of oatmeal cookies and years of canning, especially on sticky summer days when the heat intensified everything.

Oleeta's house was one of the few places I was allowed to ride my bike to, and on those stifling days, I'd fill its basket with yellow and blue Red Heart yarn and a pair of double-pointed aluminum needles. In my memory, I puff down County Road N on that bike—with swooping handlebars and a banana seat—my glasses sliding down my nose, my dirty blond hair in braids. My polyester shorts—getting a little small—creep up on my thighs. My skin sticks to the seat, and it hurts when it rips away with each rotation of the pedals. I persevere. I've adopted my mother's determination that I will learn to knit, something she never could do.

Knitting goes way back in my family, on both sides, but somehow it never trickled its way down to me. My mother's

Colorful Beginnings
A young knitter uses colored needles from two different sets to knit her first project. (Photograph © Chris Hartlove)

mother was the daughter of Czech immigrants—South Dakota pioneers—and she, like her parents, lived a hard life. She lost husbands and raised eight children, sometimes alone, on a series of northern Wisconsin farms. She knit tightly.

My father's grandfather knit also, when he was a boy and sick in bed for the entirety of a northern Minnesota winter. "You might as well be useful while you're lying there," his mother told him, probably in Danish, probably out of Scandinavian pragmatism but also the harsh reality of survival in a log cabin in the woods bordering Canada. He knit socks for his entire family that year.

But by the time I am nine, there's been a break in these knitting lines. No one in my father's family knits anymore, and my mother's mother has just died. Her last Christmas present to me was a craft book for children that featured knitting instructions among patterns for paper lilies and Popsicle-stick houses. I have tried to follow them, but I cannot make them work.

At Oleeta's, I receive an expansive smile, those eyes crinkle nearly shut, and the cardinal voice sings. I am offered lemonade or maybe ice tea; at some point we will share oatmeal cookies, but not yet. We sit closely on her scratchy couch, the fabric pricking my thighs. The windows are open, but there's no breeze, and perspiration beads lightly on her lip, pursed in concentration. She peers over her bifocals, examining my yarn and needle choices. She threads yarn through her fingers with grace, poises a needle, and begins with it a dance I recognize from a diagram in my book. It's like she's directing a tiny orchestra in her hand, but weaving yarn as she does, making stitches. I can almost hear its music in my head—if a song could be seen, could be touched, would it look like this?

With sweaty hands, I take the work she's begun. We huddle together on her couch, and she guides my fingers in looping yarn over needles, picking up stitches and pulling them through in deliberate, anxious motions. As the afternoon progresses, my stitches go from impossibly tight to ridiculously loose, creating a strip of knitting that begins narrow and rigid, then expands, then shifts to the right before straightening out. But there it is, a knitted thing, and I have made it.

Thrilled, I take it home to show my mother, unravel it all so I can demonstrate that clever business of casting on, and realize I've forgotten how. For one excruciating evening, I am unable to knit. It feels like being trapped, like

suddenly losing a friend. The next day, back at Oleeta's, she laughingly reteaches me that dance with the hands.

That year, I knit 4-H projects furiously for the Polk County Fair. I win blue ribbons on them all: a yellow headband, a blue pocketbook, a pink pincushion. For subsequent fairs, I knit scarves, pillows, a baby blanket, mittens. I learn to read patterns, and when I am fourteen—in the thick of my first crush—I knit a complicated Aran afghan while dreaming about a boy who never calls. When I am sixteen, I knit a Fair Isle sweater that wins a grand champion ribbon, but is also too big, so it never is worn.

In the years that follow, I knit through college breaks and on road trips with girlfriends. I knit myself together after a nasty breakup; I knit for a new husband. I knit for babies miscarried and babies born so robust my creations don't fit. I knit while plotting a graduate thesis; I knit to keep my hands from shaking as I watch the World Trade Center towers fall and wait for my husband to come home from midtown Manhattan. I knit sweaters that are photographed for magazines, I knit hats for Afghan refugees, I knit socks for my entire family. I knit to soothe myself; I knit when I feel lost and need some mooring; I knit when I am depressed and need some hope. I knit on the phone and in gossiping groups, but most often, I knit in silence, hypnotized by the waltz of yarn and needles, keeping time with the orchestra of thoughts in my head.

It's easy to take this gift for granted, like a loyal friend, like the woman who taught me, like a heartbeat, like breath. But while I don't like to entertain the thought, the truth is, I don't know who I would be if I couldn't knit.

Oleeta, as it happens, no longer can knit. I don't remember what year she had her accident, or what I was doing, or even where I lived. I don't remember my reaction when my mother called me, speaking as if I were a small child, in the tone she uses when imparting bad news. I remember the message: how Oleeta had been crossing a street and was hit by a car, how she was paralyzed from the neck down and would be for life, how she would need a respirator, forever, to breathe and to speak.

"When we die," my sister asked my mother when she was quite small, "what happens to the part of us that laughs and dances and sings?" When a knitter's hands are stilled, where does that creative force go? What might she have made, what has been left incomplete? Who might she have taught, what lives might she have changed? Who does she become, without her knitting to remind her? I don't remember wondering all this at the time, nor do I remember looking at my own hands, marveling in the miracle that they are, what beauty they can pull from disorder, and how so much of who I am comes from what they can do.

When I have seen Oleeta in the years since, what I notice most is that she still is soft, in all the ways I remembered, that her eyes still crinkle deeply, that she never seems to stop smiling. Her hands are the softest they've ever been. I visit her occasionally, showing her my latest project, mailing her clips of articles I've written, and always, always, thanking her for her gift to me. She's never told me that

she misses it, and it would seem cruel to ask. Maybe knitting meant something different to her than it did to me—a childhood task, a family obligation, a way to be useful. There are, after all, other things to be missed.

But maybe she still knits sometimes in her mind, in the silent spaces, weaving together thoughts and finding sense in the senseless as she, like me, conducts the orchestra in her head. Maybe the memory of knitting lingers, and with it the peace it brings, the stillness and soothing and joy, like the thrill of a childhood triumph, like a cardinal's song.

Beginner's Delight
An enthusiastic beginning knitter works her way through a bright-red seed-stitch scarf on the cover of this pattern book published by Spinnerin in 1961.

Have Yarn, Will Travel
With a couple of tangled skeins of Red Heart yarn and her dog in her bike basket, the happy teen featured on the cover of this 1950s pattern booklet is off to her next knitting lesson.

An Idyllic Scene
There is no better way to escape the worries of a hectic day than to rock and knit by the fireplace. (Photograph © J. C. Allen & Sons, Inc.)

Let's Learn to Knit
In 1966, 4-H published these three colorful guides to teach young members how to knit and purl, increase and decrease, pick up stitches and buttonholes, and create a stitch pattern.

LET'S LEARN TO KNIT
with increase and decrease

COOPERATIVE EXTENSION SERVICE ✤ OREGON STATE UNIVERSITY, CORVALLIS

Phase 3
4-H 933

LET'S LEARN TO KNIT
with pick up stitches and buttonholes

COOPERATIVE EXTENSION SERVICE ✤ OREGON STATE UNIVERSITY, CORVALLIS

EXTENSION SERVICE, KANSAS STATE UNIVERSITY, MANHATTAN

LET'S LEARN TO K
with knit and p

Phase 1
4-H 177

A Quiet Moment
Anna Neils takes a break from knitting the sleeve of a sweater to gaze out the window for a moment. (Photograph courtesy of the Minnesota Historical Society)

Knitting Dollies and Spools

In the early half of the twentieth century, mothers wrapped up wooden knitting dolly kits in pretty Christmas paper to give to daughters too young to learn how to knit with regular knitting needles. These wooden spool kits, often painted to resemble dolls, were made in Great Britain and the United States and follow the same basic concept. Young knitters-to-be looped yarn once around each of the four metal pegs that protruded from the top of the hollow spool. One by one, using a small needle that comes with the kit, knitters pulled yarn loops up over the top of the pegs, letting the loops drop into the center hole. A knitted cord eventually emerged from the base of the spool, a reward for the young knitter's persistence. Kit instructions provided countless ideas for how to use the colorful cords—make a beanie, a placemat, a belt, a potholder! With the renewed interest in knitting, knitting dolly kits are once again available through specialty knitting stores on the internet. Give it a try!

Learning to Knit:
A Romantic Tragedy in Four Acts

By Michael Dregni

Throughout his childhood, book editor and author Michael Dregni had a series of thick and woolly Norwegian sweaters to keep him warm during the coldest of Minnesota winters. When his favorite Setesdal sweater began to wear out several years ago, he had but a hint of knitting experience as he started contemplating a replacement. After the baptism by fire he relates in the following essay, he continues to knit, spending many a snowy Minnesota evening knitting in the kitchen with his wife, Sigrid. And those sweaters from his childhood are now keeping his two sons warm.

Act I: Learning Not to Knit

The story you are about to read is true. Some names have been changed to protect the innocent: We'll simply call her "my wife."

It began innocently enough. I was the proud owner of an ancient and beloved Norwegian Setesdal sweater, made for me when I was young by a Norwegian friend of the family. This lustrous blue-and-white Setesdal had kept me warm through many a Minnesota winter. It still fit fine after fifteen years, but even that wiry Rauma yarn was beginning to wear out, and the thought of perhaps losing the sweater was too much to bear. My wife was a budding knitter, self-taught and supremely obsessed, so I humbly and innocently asked her if she might maybe knit me another one.

Little did I realize what I had requested. My wife proudly informed me that one does not simply pick up some needles and a ball of yarn and start knitting a sweater every day of the week. It required *planning*.

I realized this, I replied. I had already done the planning: I wanted the sweater to be black and white.

Hah! It required more than planning, I was told—it required *engineering!* I obviously didn't understand what went into the art of knitting.

That wasn't quite true (although darn close to it). My grandmother had once taught me to knit in my long-ago youth. Backed by her never-ending patience, Grandma steered my fingers through the ballet of knitting and purling. She then loaned me some gigantic size 10 needles and pastel-yellow Red Heart yarn for me to sweat away through

Blue and White Norwegian Star Sweater
A close-up of a Norwegian star sweater designed by Solveig Hisdal reveals the intricate two-color work characteristic of this popular Norwegian knitting style. (Photograph © Solveig Hisdal)

a weekend making a scarf for my GI Joe. Ultimately, though, I should admit that she did the casting on and binding off. And I guess I should also point out that when I got bored, she did in fact supply most of the stitches in between. Still, my intentions had been good.

That brings me, ten years later, to my next knitting project. During Christmas break from college, I bravely—or brazenly—decided I was going to knit my new girlfriend a scarf. I had visions of her wearing a glorious deep-brown alpaca scarf handcrafted by me; it would be a gift no money could buy. This last part wasn't exactly true, however: My vision was inspired by a deep-brown alpaca scarf I saw at a store that bore a price tag of a mere $12. Why I didn't just buy it, I'll never know. Instead, I spent $12 on three skeins of alpaca, enlisted my mom to give me remedial knitting lessons, and then proceeded to spend my full three-week vacation slaving away. With three inches of scarf completed, a visiting aunt showed pity and offered to knit a couple rows. During a coffee break with my mom, she proceeded to knock off about a foot of scarving, and I was suddenly now about a quarter of the way around my girlfriend's neck. By the time I finally finished, I had a scarf that look like a well-used, four-foot-long dishrag. My knit stitches were as loose as a noose, my purling square-knot tight, and the result was indeed homemade. I was through with knitting for good, but proud of my product. My girlfriend seemed happy enough with the scarf, but then lost it just two weeks later. That was enough to make me lose that girlfriend.

So, I knew all about knitting and sacrifice, I told my wife. And I was ready for her to make that sacrifice, whatever it might mean to me.

But there was one further item she had not mentioned. There was an old curse, she now gravely told me: One should never knit a sweater for her husband. It was akin to opening an umbrella in the house, throwing a hat on a bed, and other folk maxims handed down through the ages. Knitting a sweater for a husband would bring bad luck.

Well, it was tough to argue with that—although I had a sneaking suspicion this age-old old-wife's tale was born only moments earlier.

Everyone Wears Red Heart Sweaters
On the back cover of this pattern book published in 1952 by J. & P. Coats-Clarks, a husband and wife dressed in matching grey cardigans and vests admire the family's colorful stash of Red Heart yarn.

With another Minnesota winter on the way, I became fixated on supplementing my sweater stock. At my wife's suggestion, I called Ingebretson's, the local Scandinavian crafts shop, giftstore, and grocery, and they directed me to a knitter who worked on contract. I was emboldened to learn her name was Ingrid Johannsdauttir or Astrid Andersson or something like that, but she too turned me down. She had given up contract knitting, she said. Money simply wasn't a fair exchange for all the labor a sweater required. Looking up from her own knitting project, my wife chorused in with a smug nod.

My wife then suggested I go shopping and just buy a damn sweater. My billfold would come out far ahead and I would have my sweater then and there, instead of waiting impatiently for months. So I went shopping. Ingebretson's had tall piles of Setesdal, Fana, and Rosekofte sweaters on the shelves, but while beautiful, they lacked something. My old Setesdal was thick and tough, some of the rows were uneven, one sleeve a tad bit longer than the other: it had that quaint quality that only homemade can have, no matter how good machine-knit sweaters are designed. I came home empty handed—and with a growing chill between my shoulder blades.

I could not find my sweater for love nor money.

Act II: Purling to Perdition

It was in the following days that my wife made her big mistake. During the autumn evenings, we'd sit around the living room after our son was in bed, me reading and she knitting. Or, I should say, I tried to read. As she knit, she talked, chatting on gaily in her knitting nirvana, telling me tales of our son's antics, happily asking me questions about the book I was supposedly reading.

Finally, I set down my book and said, "Forget it! If I can't read, I may as well join you. Teach me how to knit."

For a brief moment there she looked as if she wished she could rewind events, like unraveling some mistaken rows of knitting. Then she got a mischievous look and said, "OK. Get some needles."

Needles in hand, she then asked me what I wanted to knit. I thought this was obvious. A Setesdal sweater, of course.

She thought that hilarious, but after all the discussion of knitting Setesdal sweaters, she decided it was time for my comeuppance. I didn't remember the first thing about knitting, so she showed me how again, using a circular needle to save me from my own purling. Then she displayed how to hold and throw the two strands of different-colored yarn. I had my old Setesdal on, so I could copy the pattern to make a swatch. That, she figured, would bore me into silence.

Her reasoning proved wrong. After a day spent watching a computer, the handwork of knitting offered a long-forgotten tactile pleasure. It was restive, restorative. I was ready for more.

A Delicious Stash of Yarn
Colorful skeins of yarn once filled the shelves of Skyloom Fibers, a beloved Denver, Colorado, knitting shop that closed its doors in 1999. (Photograph © Chris Hartlove)

My swatch was done—although it was only two inches long and an inch high. I didn't have time for more as I was impatient to get started on the real deal.

My wife hesitated in setting me off on the next step, but finally she did. She helped me calculate my gauge, then steered me to her own battered copy of Elizabeth Zimmerman's *Knitting Without Tears* so I could learn sweater mathematics. After some over-quick calculations, I was set. She then asked me if I had a pattern. Sure—my old Setesdal. I'd simply copy it.

She considered this for a moment, then told me I needed yarn. As she admitted later, she figured once I tired of the project, she'd find a home for the $80 worth of skeins in her overflowing stash stored in dresser drawers, suitcases under the bed, and boxes hidden in closets.

And, as she again later admitted, she figured this project would keep me occupied and out of her hair for the next year—if not the next two or three years.

Little did she know.

Act III: A Short Time Later...

It was then that I entered a little-known and largely invisible underworld known as the yarn shop. They look innocent enough, these stores, sitting quietly in low-rent strip malls, old storefronts, or converted houses on side streets and bearing quaint names like Yarn Barn, Knit Hut, or The String of Purls. Most men and many women hardly give them a second glance, often not even realizing they're there.

Inside is another universe. The assembly of knitters—primarily women—speak a foreign language of bizarre terms—steeks and stockinette, short rows and slipping stitches—or drop into pure cryptology, such as s.1, k.1, p.s.s.o. They talk of strange goat breeds, exotic guanacos, rare rabbits, and musk ox while fingering strands of angora and cashmere and quivit as heavenly expressions spread across their faces. They study yarn cards or hold up hanks to the sunlight, eye the colors, then ooh and aah. They stand still yet travel around the world and back in time as they discuss sweater patterns and styles, from Norway to the Aran Islands, Iceland to Bolivia. Some may think knitting is "just" a hobby, but it's much more. It's a highly organized secret society rife with esoterica and arcana.

I entered this world without knowing the password. Back at Ingebretson's, I wove my way through the tatting and Hardanger embroidery supplies to the Wall of Yarn. The eyes of the little old ladies who staff the Scandinavian crafts section followed me with a kindly gaze as though I had taken a wrong turn at the herring counter. One of them stepped forward and politely asked if she could help me, probably ready to point me back to the replica Viking helmets and broadswords. But when I told her I was making a Setesdal and needed skeins of black and white yarn, I had unknowingly uttered the password and was welcomed into the secret society. She took on the role of my grandmother, loaded my arms with yarn, and I was off.

Yet before I left, she also gave me some sage words of advice. Echoing ancient wisdom about not making anything better than God's work, she said all good knitters have to be sure to knit in a mistake so their creation is not perfect. I nodded and promised I'd do my best.

Back home, my wife helped me cast on to start my first arm, gave what sounded suspiciously like a chuckle, and then promptly left town. She was off to an archaeology conference in Cincinnati for three days; I was left home with our three-year-old son, two needles, and a tangle of Peer Gynt yarn.

My son caught chicken pox the next day. This proved a benefit in disguise, however, as it allowed me to call work and report I'd be staying home for a while. Then I began knitting. When we picked up my wife at the airport three days later, my son was on the mend and I dragged along my knitting to the arrival gate—my sleeve was done and I needed her to show me how to bind off so I could use those needles to get started on the next arm.

Obsession takes many forms. Some people dress up like Vikings and reenact battles with broadswords. Others—like my wife—stockpile yarn to the point where we need a larger home. Now that I've taken up knitting, let's just say that we've come to an understanding.

Two months later, my Setesdal was done. It was a testament to obsessiveness, but I had enjoyed knitting so much that I stayed up until the wee hours, the needles clicking away, chatting with my wife as she made fine-gauge socks and flowery children's hats. Sure, my sweater was a bit lumpy under the arms where the drop-shoulders joined and yes, the body gauge wavers around a bit, leaving me plenty of room to grow into. But it's all mine.

Act IV: Meanwhile, Back at the Ranch

The first time I wore my creation in public, I was halted at the grocery store by a woman wearing her own handknit sweater. She oohed and aahed over my sweater, and then turned to my wife and asked her how long it had taken her to knit. My wife didn't know what to say and just mutely waved in my direction.

But that's really just the beginning of the story, because as soon as I finished my sweater, I used the extra skeins to start on a Setesdal for my wife, ancient curses be damned. Her sweater took an extra month or two, but by now I was such a good knitter I didn't need to even consciously knit in that one mistake the women at Ingebretson's had warned me about—it knit itself in like magic. And to my wife's and my surprise, this second sweater wasn't lumpy or misshapen. She even wears it.

Scandinavian Treasures

A vast array of Scandinavian-inspired sweaters, gloves, and caps decorate the covers of these knitting pattern books from the 1940s.

The Learn How Book

CROCHETING
KNITTING
EMBROIDERY
TATTING
HAIRPIN LACE

BOOK 345

The Needlework Arts Self-Taught

15 CENTS

Tales of a Knitting Neophyte

By Kari Cornell

Over the past few years, as knitting has become increasingly popular, knitting clubs have begun to meet in local coffee shops, college dormitories, yarn shops, or private living rooms. When friends invited writer Kari Cornell to join their club with promises of teaching her how to knit, she couldn't say no. Kari spends her days editing books and her nights cozy in her favorite chair, knitting row after row on her latest work in progress. Each month she looks forward to seeing old friends and learning a new trick or shortcut at knitting-club gatherings just like those described in this essay.

I fell into knitting rather haphazardly, with no apparent regard for the consequences. I had no idea, for instance, that knitting was habit-forming, that before long I would be unable to sit in front of the TV or ride in a car without having some sort of knitting project in my lap. No inkling that I would begin to collect skein after skein for future projects, only to let them sit, unused in the bottom of what would become—by default, really—my knitting basket. Heck, I didn't even know what a skein was! I clearly hadn't the foggiest notion of what was to come. So when my friend Amy asked if I'd be interested in joining a knitting club, I naively said yes. I mean really, a lazy Sunday afternoon in mid January, good friends, the promise of a slice of cheesecake—what could possibly be the harm in that? Best of all, Amy's friend Gigi had agreed to give lessons to the newbies.

Well, I was definitely a newbie. I laugh when I think about it now, but I was quite sure that I could not learn how to knit. No one in my immediate family is a knitter, and it seemed to me that knitting was an art one should learn at a young age, preferably under the watchful eye of a grandmother or mother. My grandmother is a superb seamstress, but she does not knit. My mother always has some sort of creative endeavor in the works. When I was growing up in the 1970s, she was hooked on macramé. Curtains, owl wallhangings, lamps, and other evidence of this phase still decorate her home. She taught me how to macramé, but she is not a knitter, and she did not teach me how to knit. So my skewed logic went something like this:

Grandmother does not knit.

Mother does not knit.

Therefore, I cannot knit.

I took this to heart and believed that, given my lineage, I was not destined to be a knitter.

Despite these overwhelming odds, I decided go to the first knitting-club meeting. First, I needed to buy yarn and needles. This seemed to me an easy enough task, but as soon as my foot crossed the threshold of my local yarn shop, I knew it would take some time—I was immediately sidetracked by the barrage of colors and textures. Yarns in rich reds, deep chocolate browns, and vibrant greens filled shelves from floor to ceiling. I was amazed by the knitted sample sweaters, scarves, and hats . . . people created these things using two sticks and some string? The concept struck me as nothing short of witchcraft—in the best of

Teach Yourself to Knit!
The Learn How Book, published by the Canadian Spool Cotton Company in 1941, promises to dispel the mysteries of crocheting, knitting, embroidery, tatting, and hairpin lace in only thirty-one pages.

possible ways, of course. After wandering around in a daze for five, ten, fifteen minutes (who can say?), I stumbled upon the wall of needles and remembered my purpose. Hmmm… a lot more choices than I had anticipated. Should I start with bamboo or aluminum, circular or straight? Double-points? What were those? I must have looked out of sorts, as it wasn't long before the woman behind the counter appeared by my side.

"Can I help you find anything?" she asked.

"I'm just learning to knit and I'd just like to buy a pair of needles and yarn to get started."

Of course she asked the obvious questions next. Did I have a pattern? What did I want to knit?

It hadn't even crossed my mind that I might need to have some idea about what I would attempt to knit in order to select needles and yarn. Couldn't she just sell me some yarn and needles and be done with it? Did I have to have an actual project or pattern in mind? That seemed like an awfully big commitment, and I didn't think I was quite ready for it. I didn't even know how to knit!

Finally I decided, with a little bit of coaxing on her part, that I could make a scarf. She pointed out a couple of yarns that would be suitable for a scarf and showed me how to read the yarn label for needle size. I selected a deep red wool and size five needles with red ends that matched the yarn (this seemed important to me at the time). Bag in hand, I headed to my first knitting lesson.

I was surprised to discover that about half of the group already knew how to knit. A couple of knitters had learned when they were younger, and only needed a refresher course. I looked upon these peers with respect, awe, and touch of envy. How much easier it would be if I were simply reacquainting myself with an old skill! Then my fingers would only have to remember rather than learn something entirely new. I'm sure Gigi, whose hands were full teaching never-even-held-a-pair-of-knitting-needles neophytes the very basics, was relieved to have a few once-upon-a-time knitters in the room.

Holding knitting needles in my hands for the first time was downright awkward. I imagine this was what it must have been like to learn to stand, balance, and then step across a room on my own two feet; eat with a fork; or peddle a bicycle without training wheels. Even picking up rice with chopsticks seemed easier than this! But I kept at it, and by the end of our first knitting-club meeting I had learned how

to cast on and how to knit. I left that first meeting a little spacey after spending the past few hours staring intently at the needles, ribbed with loops of the red yarn, and mentally exhausted from trying to process the basics of knitting, but thrilled nonetheless. I was learning how to knit!

Little did I know that I would have to relearn casting on and the knit stitch at our February club meeting, as the skills quickly faded from my memory without practice during the intervening weeks. This wasn't such a big deal, though, and I even added purling to my limited repertoire during that second meeting. By March, however, it was just plain embarrassing to have to ask for help with knitting and purling again. So I planted myself on the floor in the craft section of the local bookstore and perused the knitting books, looking for a set of diagrams and instructions I could understand. I settled on *The Knitting Workbook* by Debbie Bliss and headed home to figure out this knitting thing once and for all.

In the comfort of my living room, I readied myself for the task at hand, settling into my favorite armchair with a mug of hot tea and The Book by my side. Before I get too far into this, let me explain that I am very much a text person, so I began my study by doing what was most logical—reading the text. But as much as I tried to translate the words into the act, the directions refused to make sense. So I studied the yarn on the needles and compared what I held in my hands to the diagrams in the book. I knew just enough to realize that what I was doing was *not* knitting. My enthusiasm began to fade. The diagrams, which seemed very clear as I studied them at the bookstore, were of no help. Then I had an idea.

My husband, Brian, sat innocently watching TV from the couch nearby. He had never knit a stitch in his life, but as a graphic designer, he is much better at understanding visuals than I am. If you could have only seen him at that moment, you would know exactly what I mean—his eyes were glued to the TV screen.

"Have you figured it out?" he asked, without looking my way.

"No, but I have an idea. Would you take a look at these diagrams and see if you can make sense of them?"

Brian is also one of the best problem-solvers I know; he wasted no time. He picked up the needles, studied the diagrams, and in less than a minute he had knit his first stitch. He knit another as I watched closely. Aha! That's it!

Now I could do this. Knitting two stitches is apparently not enough to fall under the bewitching spell of the craft, so Brian more than willingly handed over the needles and yarn. My hands moved clumsily at first, but soon enough I was picking up speed. I was determined to knit my bit before the April meeting.

Through the spring and into the summer, knitting-club days came and went as more and more of the red wool scarf emerged from my needles. Not content to just knit in stockinette, I experimented with different stitch patterns, knocking off a couple of rows of seed stitch, switching to garter stitch, and then purling for a while. The scarf began to look kind of cool, especially to a novice knitter like me. I thought it looked so good, in fact, that I began to show it to friends and relatives.

"Look, I knit this," I would chirp "Can you believe it?"

"Yes, I most certainly can," I mutter sarcastically as I hold this attempt at a scarf in my hands today, "And don't tell me, you learned to knit only yesterday, right?"

Yikes! That scarf was a tangled mess. Somewhere along the way (about two inches in, to be precise), I began to inadvertently add stitches at the end of the rows. What was originally a nice seven-inch-wide garment grew to a ten-inch-wide abomination. About the time I realized that my scarf was no longer cool, I didn't have the heart to rip down to where I had started to increase, and the thought of dismantling it altogether just felt wrong. I stuck it out for another week or so, and then abandoned the project, tossing it into the bottom of my knitting basket, where it has remained ever since.

Two and a half years, several baby hats, three mittens, and two sweaters later, I've finally reached the point where I think I could rip apart the aborted scarf without a sense of remorse. In fact, the idea appeals to me more and more each day, especially since I've started to eye the fetching red wool as a prime candidate for a pair of felted mits . . . the perfect project after I finish the baby hat, knit the seven skeins of Lopi piled in my closet into a sweater, and figure out what to do with the bundle of lavender mercerized cotton sitting in the bottom of my knitting basket.

Knitter's Stash
This basket, bathed in diffused sunlight and overflowing with soft-colored skeins and neatly worked swatches, will surely tempt any passing knitter. (Photograph © Chris Hartlove)

One Row at a Time . . .
A young woman takes advantage of a few precious moments to knit a few rows on her latest project. (Photograph courtesy of the Library of Congress)

Learn to Knit

this sure easy way

1 • TO CAST ON
Make a slip loop on left-hand needle. Insert point of right-hand needle from left to right into this loop. With the right hand, carry the wool from the ball under and around the right-hand needle.

2 • TO CAST ON
Draw the point of right-hand needle, with the wool around it, through the loop.

3 • TO CAST ON
Insert the point of left-hand needle from right to left into this newly made loop. Withdraw right-hand needle.

4 • TO CAST ON
*Insert point of right-hand needle between the last two loops made on left-hand needle; carry wool under and around the point of right-hand needle. Make the new loop and transfer it to left-hand needle as before. Repeat from * until required number of stitches are on left-hand needle.

1 • TO KNIT
Hold the needle, with the stitches to be knitted, in left hand with the wool from ball away from you. *Insert point of right-hand needle from left to right into front of first stitch on left-hand needle. With right hand, bring wool from ball under and around point of right-hand needle.

2 • TO KNIT
Draw the point of the right-hand needle, with the wool around it, forward through the loop on the left-hand needle.

3 • TO KNIT
Slip the worked loop off the left-hand needle and keep newly made loop on right-hand needle. Repeat from * for required number of knit stitches, as given in pattern.

1 • TO PURL
Hold the needle, with the stitches to be purled, in the left hand with the wool from the ball toward you. *Insert point of the right-hand needle from right to left into front of first stitch on left-hand needle. With right hand, bring wool from ball over and around point of right-hand needle.

2 • TO PURL
Draw the point of the right-hand needle, with the wool around it, back through the loop on the left-hand needle.

3 • TO PURL
Slip the worked loop off left-hand needle and keep the newly worked loop on right-hand needle. Repeat from * for required number of purl stitches given in pattern.

1 • TO CAST OFF
To cast off knit stitches: Knit 2 sts. *Insert left-hand needle from left to right through the first stitch knitted.

2 • TO CAST OFF
Draw this stitch over other stitch and off right-hand needle. Knit another stitch from left-hand needle and repeat from * until all stitches have been worked from left-hand needle and only one stitch remains on right-hand needle.
Break wool and draw it through last loop. To cast off purl stitches: Purl stitches from left-hand needle instead of knitting them.

Look and Learn
Vintage pattern books, knitting instruction books, and contemporary knitting magazines often publish diagrams reminding readers how to knit, purl, cast on, and cast off. Rhymes may help knitters remember the process too—under the fence, catch the sheep, back we come, off we leap.

Knit-Surfing the Subway

by Suzyn Jackson

Knitters are a determined bunch. When their fingers itch with the urge to knit, you can bet the knitter will find a way, no matter where they may be or how great the challenge. Although this story isn't about learning to knit for the first time, it is about mastering the art of knitting on the crowded and sometimes lurching New York City subway—not an easy task! Author Suzyn Jackson is an aspiring New York City artist who writes, knits, and designs jewelry. She holds a B.A. from Amherst College and is currently studying at the Fashion Institute of Technology in New York. Her passions include fine art, Dumas, the southeast corner of Central Park, and red socks.

It takes a lot to get noticed on the New York City subway. Simply talking to yourself won't cut it. In fact, you can sing along to your iPod™, make out with your sweetie, or scream at your dead mother without raising an eyebrow. Wearing something slinky, tight, *and* revealing might get you some glances, but they're the kind of glances that make you want to go home and take a shower. Wearing eight-inch platform boots, waist-long dreds, several dozen piercings, and/or a shaman's cape won't get you any attention whatsoever.

Well, I got noticed. People stared at me, mesmerized. Perfect strangers started up conversations, told me about their families. What was I doing to get all this attention? I was knitting.

It started about a year ago, when I had a lot of Christmas love to spread around and not much cash. I decided to make scarves for twelve people—a bit of love to wrap around their necks for the cost of two balls of yarn. Twelve scarves. Six weeks.

Now, like most people, I barely had time to get to work, do the laundry, eat dim sum, buy groceries, get together with friends, make dinner, pick up the dry cleaning, kiss my husband, and fall into bed before I had to get up and start all over again. There simply weren't enough hours in the day for regular life, never mind my own personal Santa's workshop.

There was one hour I could spare, though—the hour I spent on the subway to and from work every day. A simple and elegant solution: I'd knit on the subway.

Knitting on the subway during rush hour isn't simple, I found. And it's *way* not elegant. You can't knit sitting down—there's barely enough room to squeeze yourself in

Knit-Surfing the Subway
Author Suzyn Jackson demonstrates her method for maintaining her balance while knitting on the New York City subway. Hint: It's all in the positioning of the feet. (Photograph © Alvaro Gonzalez)

Knitting in Close Quarters
Short or circular needles are a must when knitting in a crowded subway car. (Photograph © Alvaro Gonzalez)

without flapping your elbows about. And you can't knit and hold on to a pole at the same time. Christmas loomed. So I came up with a technique I like to call "Knit-Surfing." Here's how it works:

The stance is all-important: legs spread wide, feet parallel, knees slightly bent. Hang your purse and bag over one shoulder, your knitting bag over the other, for balance. Now here's the key: stand at a 45 degree angle to the train (i.e., if the train is going S, face SE). This way, whether the train lurches from side to side (which is guaranteed on the 6 between 105th and 96th) or the conductor makes an abrupt stop (which is guaranteed at least once on every trip) you will have enough stability to stay upright.

There are space issues. Use shorter or circular needles, to avoid poking people—they don't like that. They also don't like having needles clacking in their faces, so lean back slightly to give yourself more personal space in front.

Finally the project itself must be carefully considered. Scarves are perfect—they're lightweight, you can tuck the end into your knitting bag, and you never have to look at a pattern. Looking at a pattern is not an option. Using more than one color is an option. It's a challenge, but it will get you extra points with your spectators.

Because you will have spectators. Some will never say a word, just staring, hypnotized by the needles. Some will ask you how long you've been knitting, how you learned, whether it's hard. One lady will pull out the baby blanket she's crocheting for her sister's third baby, due in March. You may get into Knit-Surfing for the thrill of multitasking, but you'll stay for the old-fashioned Christmastime Peace on Earth Goodwill towards the crochet lady.

The scarves were a big hit. My hands ached for most of January, so I went back to reading on the subway. It's kind of lonely now—no one strikes up a conversation any more, even if we're reading the same issue of the *New Yorker*. It's hard to get noticed on the subway.

I guess I'll just have to start this year's Christmas gifts early.

The Knit-Pick is the ideal gadget for all knitting and crocheting fans, especially those who like to knit in transit.

The Fleisher Yarns

"EVERY COLOR IN THE RAINBOW"

A day and a half—and this Lovely Sweater is finished!

Just follow these simple instructions:

MATERIALS: Fleisher's Shetland Floss, 8 balls Rose No. 35; 1 pair needles, No. 5.

Cast on 60 stitches. Knit plain for 1 inch. Then knit 1 row, purl 1 row, for 4 inches. Next row—drop every third stitch. (Before unravelling the dropped stitches, darn a thread through the first row of ribbing.) Next row—increase 1 stitch every second stitch. Knit plain for 8 inches. Cast on 10 stitches each side of work, 6 times. Then knit 36 rows (or 18 ribs) even. Next row—knit 91 stitches, bind off 18, knit 91. On the last 91 stitches, knit 6 rows. Next row—cast on 15 stitches on the neck-end of the work. Knit 42 rows (21 ribs) from the shoulder. Bind off 10 stitches 6 times. Knit even until front opening measures 7 inches. Make the other front to correspond. Join to the first front. Knit plain for 1 inch. Knit one row, purl 1 row, for 4 inches. Bind off, dropping every third stitch.

CUFFS: Pick up 30 stitches at the end of the sleeve. Knit 1 row, purl 1 row, for 1½ inches. Drop every third stitch. Knit 1 inch plain. Bind off.

BELT: Cast on 25 stitches. Knit 54 inches. Bind off. Sew to the front of sweater, leaving ends loose to tie.

COLLAR: Pick up the stitches from one end of the lapel to the other. Knit plain for 2 inches. Knit 1 row, purl 1 row, for 1½ inches. Drop every third stitch. Knit 1 inch plain. Bind off.

ONLY 8 balls of Fleisher's Shetland Floss and less than two days' time—that's all you need to make this delightful summer sweater. A Paris model with just that "something" in style which the French call *chic*. Think of it!—so charming a sweater, yet so economical of both time and yarn! Why not get the yarn *today?*

THE Fleisher Knitting and Crochet Manual illustrates many other exclusive sweaters as original in design as the one pictured on this page, with full directions for making each sweater. On sale at any store where The Fleisher Yarns are sold, or at bookstores and stationers everywhere. 40c. S. B. & B. W. Fleisher, Inc., Dept. 2414, Philadelphia, Pa.

N. B. There is a Fleisher Yarn of Correct Weight for Every Knitting and Crocheting Use.

The Diane Sweater
AN EXCLUSIVE FLEISHER DESIGN

CHAPTER 2

THE YARN SHOP AND BEYOND

THE LOCAL KNITSHOP, OWNED AND RUN BY SOPHIE, ALSO PROVIDED PLENTY OF CHATTER AND WOOL, WHICH FOR ME WAS ESPECIALLY USEFUL AND BEGUILING. I SPENT MORNING AFTER MORNING IN THERE MEETING LOCAL KNITTERS, DROPPING LITTLE HINTS ON THEM, AND, BEST OF ALL, ABSORBING THEIR HINTS.

–*Elizabeth Zimmermann, Knitting Around, 1989*

Cozy and Warm
This bundle of skeins in warm, complementary tones invites knitters to cast on and create a sweater using these colors. (Photograph © Solveig Hisdal)

The yarn shop is the knitter's candy store. Yarns in endless colors and blends stack shelves from floor to ceiling, tempting shoppers to sample one or two or three of the sweet skeins for their next project. Chenille, cashmere, and angora blends softly whisper from the walls, begging passers-by to touch them, while wool and cotton blends offer a dizzying array of colors, ripe for picking off the shelves.

But there's more to a yarn shop than meets the eye; it is the yarn-shop owners and employees that make one or another shop places to return to again and again. These yarn aficionados brim with knowledge, holding the answers to your most difficult knitting dilemma. Yarn shops are really places of respite, where knitters can turn with confidence when they run into snags along the way. Many knitters have a favorite local yarn shop, where they've come to know the shopkeepers or have met other knitting enthusiasts through shop-run knitting clubs. The essays collected in this chapter touch on some aspect of the yarn shop, whether it's the yarn that lines the shelves, the spinners who turn out the wool, or the people who bring life to the place.

A Rainbow of Yarns
This advertisement for Fleisher Yarns, printed in the April 1921 issue of the Ladies Home Journal, not only promotes the color choices available, it includes a pattern to knit the sweater worn by the model in the photograph.

So Begins a Fetish

By Lela Nargi

At some point or another, most knitters can attest to falling under the tantalizing spell of the yarn shop. One look at the luscious skeins in a rainbow of colors and it becomes easy to justify purchasing enough of that stunning red Lopi to make a sweater for Dad. Of course, you probably already have one or two projects in the works, but you'll get to this yarn sooner or later, right? Yarns piled in the sale bin are especially enticing.

In "So Begins a Fetish," Lela Nargi succumbs to the temptation of a yarn sale in her neighborhood as she leaves her apartment one morning to buy a loaf of bread for breakfast. This excerpt originally appeared in her book Knitting Lessons: Tales from the Knitting Path, *published by Putnam in 2003. Lela lives, writes, and knits in Brooklyn, New York.*

I stumbled upon the beginnings of a yarn sale one morning when I'd rolled out of bed and onto the street to buy a loaf of bread for breakfast. I stood on the corner, rubbing my eyes in disbelief, as boxes and boxes and boxes of yarn were hauled out of a neighborhood handknit shop and unceremoniously plunked onto the concrete. It was only 9 AM on a Saturday and there weren't many other people out and about, yet; I was the very first, and very lucky, patron of the day. As I stepped up to the cheerful little wool, my heart began to race with anticipation.

Funny–*strange*–how quickly other people materialized on the so recently deserted streets, as though some psychic channel for all yarn junkies within a five mile radius had somehow yawned open. As I pawed through the boxes, I could feel a small crowd gathering behind me. Several members of the assembly approached and began to rummage alongside me. I picked up my pace, catching my breath, gritting my teeth, and grabbing for anything that looked, in my mounting concern that someone would beat me to *the best* ball of wool, even marginally soft or colorful. I tucked potential worthies into my armpits, then under my chin,

then into the waistband of my pants. I dug and dug, every once in a while casting a quick glance upward, to see what goodies were currently being carted out of the shop (large cones, then sweater remnants), and to monitor the actions of my fellow shoppers.

With balls of yarn looped, finally, onto my fingers and no place else to hold them, I waddled up to the check-out table. Just in time. The yarn, not to be contained a moment longer, exploded off my body in every direction. The woman behind the register collected them into a neat pile and gave me a dubious look. I smiled back at her, trying to show her that I was respectable. I discovered a stray ball of wool down my shirt, plucked it out, and laid it demurely on the table. The woman tallied up my haul. $70. Was that all? I opened my wallet and discovered: I had no money.

More and more shoppers were assembling, and I could see a few of them eyeing my stash. "Don't worry," said the woman. "I'll watch it for you until you get back." I thanked her, but didn't quite trust her promise. As fast as I could, I ran for Pedro's Grocery, the nearest shop with an ATM. Closed. I ran another block to the Mini Mall, where the ATM

Cascade of Color
Naturally dyed wools in subdued, rich colors await fiber enthusiasts at La Lana Wools in Taos, New Mexico. (Photograph © Chris Hartlove)

happened to be broken. Panicked, and out of breath, I dragged myself three blocks back in the opposite direction to Superior Market, and finally—finally—dispensed myself a wad of crisp twenties. Exhausted, now, I plodded back to the yarn sale. As I trudged, I began to ask myself, "Can I really afford to spend $70 on mismatched balls of yarn? Will I ever really use half a skein of lime-and-white wool? And if so, for *what*?" Thus it happened that I was a calmer, more reasonable woman by the time I returned to the check-out table. I picked slowly through my pile, weeding. Each ball of wool I set to the side was snatched in a flash by one of a circling brood of yarn vultures.

At last, I settled on a $10 bag of caramel-colored blended wool; a ball of nubby, chocolatey merino; and another ball of merino, in butter yellow. My purchases packed neatly

Knit Better with Newlands
An advertisement from the 1940s promises knitters will have great results if they knit their next project using Newlands yarn.

into a shopping bag, and 12 new dollars handed happily over for their exchange, I did feel almost respectable as I ambled casually back home, leaving a seething, frenzied mob in my wake.

It didn't take long for me to realize that I would never use the contents of the $10 bag of blended wool I'd bought at the sale. So tantalizing when I was in the throes of the yarn jones—and starving before breakfast to boot—once I was home and fed, its patina of caramel revealed itself to be no color so luscious. What I had on my hands here were 10 balls of mucousy-looking stuff—beige with a sickly tinge of pink—that made my skin appear sallow when I held it against my arm. Included in the bag were a few practice swatches and the back panel of an abandoned sweater; apparently, someone else before me had had the same, disgruntled, reaction.

Still, I was loathe to admit an error in judgement. "Ten balls for $10," I chanted in my most delighted (feigned), bargain hunter's voice to my husband, who looked decidedly nonplussed. I squirreled the bag away in the closet, where it cluttered up my shoe corner for several weeks. Then, quietly, I moved it to the outer hallway, the last stop in our household before ultimate discarding.

I was still enthusiastic about the two balls of merino, though. Some of the brown yarn (thankfully still chocolatey-looking when contemplated post-breakfast) I set straight to working into squares, following directions in a Barbara Walker pattern treasury that I'd borrowed from my friend Elanor. Lozenge, a simple knit/purl pattern of "some antiquity," according to the book, knitted up into a squirmy-looking patch—like worms on dirt, I decided. Squared Check, which I realized too late required me to double the suggested multiple in order to achieve the full force of its geometric effect, was similarly unthrilling. So much for the brown merino. But whether the drab swatching results were honestly the fault of the wool—rather than my fault, for picking patterns inappropriate to the material—I didn't even bother to contemplate; once disappointment leads to disinterest there's no recovering from it. I cast the yarn, and the swatches it had spawned, into a deep drawer.

But I had a very particular plan for the butter yellow ball. My favorite sweater was (is) a short, V-necked cardigan made of dark grey cashmere. After three years of wear, I had finally succeeded in loving it almost to death: holes had been eaten out of it by both my elbows, and around the holes, the fabric was threadbare. I could not conceive of discarding this most perfect of all the world's sweaters; I needed to rescue it, give it a second life. Elbow patches struck me as just the thing.

Elanor, visiting for dinner one night, talked me out of knitting them. "What you want to do," she said, "is make your patches out of crochet." She rummaged around in her pocketbook and—Why? How? —emerged from it with a crochet hook. Too stunned to comment, I went to retrieve the yarn. With some hasty strokes, Elanor looped together a narrow chain, then handed the whole hook-and-wool operation over to me. I sat on a stool in my kitchen as dinner bubbled on the stove, and Elanor leaned on the counter sipping wine and monitoring my progress, and in less than half an hour, I'd finished a three-inch oval. Easy. Or at least, I thought it was.

The next day, I tried a second patch on my own. It developed into a shriveled specimen that I quickly unraveled. My next attempt wasn't any more successful. I called Elanor, who told me to widen my increases—pick up more stitches—at the curves. I did, and the resulting, third patch was . . . not bad.

The moment of truth: sewing the patches to the sweater. As I stitched, it became increasingly impossible to get the patches to lie flat. Furthermore, the yellow merino was a far sight thicker than the cashmere of my sweater, and the mingling of the two fabrics was decidedly ungainly. I finished sewing the patches on anyway, convincing myself that I was imagining things, that the patches—nice, even spirals of warm yellow—added a touch of panache to my beloved cardigan. Once I tried the thing on, though, there was no denying the obvious: the patches protruded from my elbows like perfect, perky nipples.

I resolved to wear the sweater anyway, always with my elbows bent to fill the contours of the patches. The yellow merino, which I'd planned to stash away with its brown cousin at the bottom of a drawer, met another, albeit accidental, fate: between the claws of my cat. Thereafter, I vowed I would steel myself against the siren song of the Yarn Sale. A large shopping bag of remnants, oddly-colored skeins, displeasingly textured balls, and wooly misfits of every variety is testament to the breadth of my failure.

Handknit Flower Garden

Solveig Hisdal drew inspiration for this beautifully knitted flower, variations of which are featured in many of her sweater designs, from a painting on the inside of a wooden chest exhibited at the Vestvågøy Museum in Norway. (Photograph © Solveig Hisdal)

Endless Possibilities
Sample swatches in a multitude of stitch and color patterns show just a few of the possibilities available to knitters today. (Photograph © Chris Hartlove)

Knitting Companion
In this quaint Russian postcard, a young woman keeps one eye on her knitting and the other on her cat, who looks about ready to pounce on the next free strand of yarn.

Lily Chin's Top 10 Ways to Hide the Stash

Knit designer Lily M. Chin, author of *Knit and Crochet with Beads, The Urban Knitter,* and *Mosaic Magic: Afghans Made Easy,* has a few ideas about what to do with all of that extra yarn. This list first appeared in an interview with Lily Chin, posted on the *Knitter's* magazine website.

1. Tape a bag of yarn to the underside of all the chairs—who'll know???

2. Put a slipcover over a bag of yarn, stick it on the couch, call it a pillow.

3. Remove the cushions of the couch, stuff with yarn instead.

4. There are narrow books that don't reach all the way to the back of the bookshelf. That dead space behind such books is good for several skeins.

5. Do you wear ALL your shoes at the same time? No, stick a skein of yarn in each unworn shoe (boots are great for this very reason).

6. Everyone has clothes in the closet that are never, ever worn. Sew up the bottoms of the garments, insert yarn. Do not forget to sew up bottoms of sleeves. There's enough in each sleeve for more than a bag's worth.

7. Never cook, only order take-out or go to restaurants. You've now got the whole oven!

8. Look to the china cabinet. That large soup tureen? Maybe a bag. Large teapot? A few balls. Covered dish? The same.

9. The freezer is advantageous for fuzzies such as angora or mohair. Make sure to place in plastic bag first. This is known as the high-fiber diet!

10. Get a really large box and fill it up with lots and lots of yarn. Put a tablecloth over it. Voila, instant table (but you can't get your feet underneath it).

The Accidental Spinner, or Husband Discovers Wheel

by Naomi Dagen Bloom

If a never-ending supply of yarn is every knitters dream, Naomi Dagen Bloom's dreams came true the day her husband, Ron, took up spinning. Now Naomi knits with the wool he spins! "The Accidental Spinner, or Husband Discovers Wheel," traces Ron Bloom's journey from accompanying Naomi on yarn-seeking missions as an innocent bystander to developing a genuine interest in spinning wool. Ron is a woodworker and Naomi is an environmental and performance artist. They live on the twenty-first floor of a New York City apartment building. To learn more about the "Knit One Red Worm" project mentioned in the essay, visit www.Cityworm.com.

This is a twenty-first century love story about old people. Not the kind where an eighty-seven-year-old woman becomes a fatal attraction for a twenty-five-year-old man. Our tale is old-fashioned, appealing to those who know that "the long-term happy marriage" still exists. Ron and I are not an adorable old couple who keep our voices low and always agree. How, I ask, can he be such a mellow spinner and still watch a football game on TV at the same time? Obligingly, he turns the sound off and we spin and knit in the same room.

We arrived at this idyllic yarn situation through the many trips we've taken around the world in search of the perfect red yarn. Ron has always been an enthusiastic companion on my fiber searches. A few years ago, I was deep into an environmental art project in an effort to attract public attention to the wonders of kitchen composting. In Teotitlan, a small rug-making village outside Oaxaca,

Mexico, the sight of vibrant, red cochineal-dyed wool drying in the sun made me think of the red wiggler worms composting in my kitchen, and gave me a great idea. I hadn't knit for many years, but I used the wool to knit red worms of all sizes. What began as a simple stockinette tube grew into a 150-worm installation, including worms from more than 110 fiber artists from around the world. The worms hung from the rafters of a greenhouse in New York City to honor the red wiggler worms that eat food waste and produce compost.

While in Mexico, I met an American who showed me a newspaper article about a quirky Englishman living in Ocotlan, another small village near Oaxaca, who had developed a mohair spinning factory by reusing nineteenth-century equipment. I was surprised by how intrigued Ron was with the Englishman's ingenuity of updating the old technology to produce a finer Mexican mohair. Looking

Carding and Spinning

Tulalip women card and spin wool on the front porch of their home on the Tulalip Indian Reservation in the state of Washington, 1898. (Photograph courtesy of the University of Washington Libraries, Special Collections, NA1539)

A Little Sheepish
Master knitter Elizabeth Zimmermann was fond of saying that knitting has been around since the beginning of sheep. (Photograph © Marilyn Nosewicz)

back, I realize that this was the beginning of Ron's interest in spinning and fiber. I saw the project as yet another means to obtain a uniquely textured red yarn for knitting worms.

The following year we went to China, where we scoured small shops in Beijing and huge department stores in Shanghai for red yarn heavier than sportweight. But all the yarn—even in villages along the Yangtze River—was the same. Many women knit in public throughout China, following intricate patterns without instructions while they tend their shops or sell souvenirs near the Great Wall. But in all the stores I found only one weight in two brands (Chang Jiang brand being most prominent) and only a few colors—gold, yellow, and red.

With the worm-knitting project completed, I turned to personal things. I knit a corncob baby bunting in cotton yarn for our first grandchild. Soon after, a trip to Prince Edward Island and Nova Scotia stimulated thoughts of handspun and hand-dyed yarn. Many Canadians continue these labor-intensive crafts. Our family, too, had always enjoyed making things "from scratch"—Ron is a woodworker, our son is a potter, and I am a knitter. Wanting to

support similar efforts in our own country, Ron and I were thrilled to learn about the New York Sheep and Wool Festival in Rhinebeck, which was only a two-hour drive upstate from our Manhattan apartment.

It was a damp and gray day when we arrived in Rhinebeck. Ron, with his ever-present camera over his shoulder, was happy to wander the fairgrounds and watch 4-H events while I went to a felting workshop. On the drive to the festival, Ron told a friend traveling with us about an especially fond memory of hitchhiking through Scotland in the 1960s. "On a one-track road in the northern Scottish hill country, I came over a rise and there was this sea of whiteness in a field ahead. I was such a city guy that it took me a minute or two to take in what I saw—endless animals, white sheep, penned in, waiting to be sheared." The shearers and shepherds, eager to have Ron take photos, invited him to climb over the fence so he could touch the fleece and smell the lanolin. At the end of his trip on the Isle of Skye he bought a loosely knit tan wool sweater that still smelled of lanolin. Much used and with a few holes, it was reluctantly handed over to Goodwill only a few years ago.

Later in the day when I caught up with Ron at the festival, he did not talk about shooting photos. He had a new idea.

"Saw this woman spinning angora from a rabbit sitting in her lap! Then I saw a chakra—means 'wheel' in Sanskrit—spinning wheel like Gandhi used in India." Then he told me he'd like to spin on one of those. Ron. Spin. This was definitely a departure. Well, maybe, I agreed, but not sitting on the ground, cross-legged; he needed something more suited to a sixty-something American man. The search began. Someone in my knitting circle would probably have ideas for Ron's next steps.

My primary knitting circle (retirement allows time for multiples!) meets every week in a Starbucks on Manhattan's Upper West Side. We push together several two-person, round tables so twenty-plus knitters can meet and shout over the background music.

When I asked about spinning, Nancy D. seemed to be the best resource, with her shoulder tattoo, bright-red hair, and history of alternative life in the far West.

"Just so you know, cotton is hard to spin—short fibers. You really want to knit cotton all the time?" Nancy asked.

Hand-Dyed Yarns
Hand-dyed yarns from Mountain Colors, a company based in Montana's Bitterroot Valley, add brilliant color to this ordinary fencepost. (Photograph © Chris Hartlove)

The Shearing Team
A pair of sheep farmers work together to shear one of the sheep in their herd. To use these old-fashioned shears, one person must turn the power crank while the other shears the sheep. (Photograph © J. C. Allen & Sons, Inc.)

No, the baby bunting had been enough, I replied. Now wool and other animal fibers were my choice.

Jen, founder of the circle, began a series of circle-wide enthusiasms, "What an incredible source of exotic yarn!"

More practical thoughts had been on my mind; I saw Ron's spinning as an excellent way to control my frequent urge to buy too much yarn (a.k.a. stash). Nancy's advice was that Ron start with drop-spindle lessons and she sent me to the website for Countrywool.com—again in upstate New York. It would be a better world if more of our dilemmas were addressed with as much attention and caring as the women provide in the Upper West Side Knit Circle.

A mammoth snowstorm almost delayed Ron's first les-

Got Your Goat
A Shady Grove Farm goat awaits its turn under the shears.
(Photograph © Naomi Dagen Bloom)

son with Claudia Krisinski in Hudson, New York. Eager to begin, Ron was not deterred. He drove the two hours each way, arriving back at our apartment more enthusiastic than ever.

"Look at this!" he shouted as he held out a lumpy white ball.

I was impressed. With a very basic drop spindle (two CDs and a stick), he had created a ball of yarn from a fuzzy pile of fleece.

Subtle change came into our lives. Most evenings Ron would pull out some fleece and begin to spin—and watch a game on TV. It was a bit disconcerting. What had I expected? He was still a twenty-first century man, even though he was into a craft more ancient than my knitting. Even his racquetball partners were impressed, though puzzled.

As winter ended, Ron announced that he wanted to look into buying a spinning wheel. Being the primary web researcher in our partnership, I quickly discovered that New York City was not the place to learn spinning or buy a wheel. But I did turn up another travel adventure. Outside of the five boroughs there is much energy devoted to the ancient art of spinning—more than 200 spinning guilds thrive in seven states. At Sally'sPlace.com, a recipe and travel newsletter, we connected with Shady Grove Farm in Apex, North Carolina. Sally herself had spent a weekend on this compact, two-acre farm with eight sheep and a nanny goat. Ron and I had an opportunity for a total yarn experience, from spinning and dyeing the wool to knitting it. And, as luck would have it, bad weather in North Carolina had delayed the yearly shearing, so Ron would once again be able to indulge in his favorite spectator sport, providing there was sunshine.

Our hosts, Dirk and Judy Tysmans, seemed to be a younger version of ourselves, at ease with shifting roles. Dirk, a computer expert, was also a good cook and he prepared a Dutch dish he had learned in his mother's kitchen. While Judy, a public health nurse, gave us yarn instruction, he took on other household tasks, including laundry. Dirk was also very involved in raising their sheep.

In his first try on Friday night, it was clear that Ron and a spinning wheel were meant for one another.

"This is great!" he announced on his initial encounter

with a Fricke spinning wheel. The next morning brought sun and a much anticipated event at Shady Grove—the shearing of eight Romney sheep and one nanny goat (angora). John, the shearer from the farm down the road, arrived at breakfast time and brought us the freshest eggs we'd ever had. Dressed in jeans and heavy shoes, Ron and I were ready. While Ron learned how to hold a sheep for shearing, I focused on documenting it all with my camera, Ron's camera, and the Tysmans' digital.

Suddenly I was whacked. What was that? Whacked again, I stumbled a bit. Nora, the nannygoat had escaped from the holding pen, and I was in her way. My only disappointment was that Ron had been too busy to grab his camera out of my hands and take a photo. Everything moved quickly, and before we knew it, four sheep were sheared. The shearers placed the large coats, still in one piece, on a screen mounted over two sawhorses. With other visitors who had come to see the shearing, I trimmed the edges of the coats, removing the parts that had been closest to the ground when on the animal. This is the true dirty work of the whole process. And then the rain came.

The unshorn animals were moved into the barn and work continued. Though wet, Ron was having a wonderful time, "Just like Scotland!" The sun returned in time for the biggest challenge—holding onto Nora, the goat, to shear her angora coat.

Saturday evening brought another delicious, Dirk-made dinner and more spinning for Ron on Majacraft and Lendrum wheels. Judy was an encouraging and thoughtful teacher. My husband, the accidental spinner, was on a roll. In between guiding Ron, Judy explained what I needed to know about knitting with handspun rather than commercially produced yarn.

On Sunday we learned to ply the yarn Ron had spun—merino wool, silk, cotton, dog hair—into two-ply skeins using the musically named tool, the Niddy Noddy, to wind a skein. Judy even demonstrated some stovetop fiber dyeing using some of the wool and silk. In the late afternoon, totally energized by our experiences, we packed up to leave. But not before Judy remembered that I'd wanted to take some red wiggler worms from her garden back to my apartment compost box! I used the small skein of Ron's finished yarn to knit him a headband as we drove back to New York. (He models it on my website.) We returned home with brown fleece from Gideon, one of the sheep on the Tysmans' farm. It's quite special to "know" the animal whose coat you're spinning and knitting. Later that spring, Ron tried out and purchased his very own wheel at the Maryland Sheep and Wool Festival. He chose an inexpensive, very workable, unglamorous "starter." Called Babe's wheel and made from PVC pipe, it was easy to put

From Sheep to Sweater
Knit designer Kristin Nicholas and her husband, Mark, model two of her creations as they watch over their flock of sheep. (Photograph © Chris Hartlove)

Knitting and Spinning
With puddles at their feet after an Oregon rainstorm, designer Lynne Vogel and her friend and collaborator Sandy Sitzman knit and spin together in the back yard. (Photograph © Chris Hartlove)

together and it takes up little room in our apartment.

So many knitters are envious when they hear that my husband spins the yarn I knit that I've considered starting a support group—"Your Spouse Could be Yarn Dependent Too!" At the first meeting, women fiber artists could develop strategies to convince their mates that there would be great financial savings if the men learned how to spin. Next, a session just for men—popcorn and beer on tap, big screen TV playing Jets versus Giants—where they quiz each other on who knows more about fiber and the technology of spinning wheels. Visualize retired men (with wives who are dedi-

cated knitters, crocheters, or weavers) as they learn what Ron calls the "highly meditative" art of spinning. Imagine a return to our earliest civilized days, only now the guys are talking "ply, tension, carding . . . quivit," along with "touchdown, lineups, Red Sox."

On a more grounded note, my physician recently told me that one theory about why women live longer than men is women are "hard-wired" to have a significant role in passing along child-raising information to their daughters. But there's no equivalent for older men. Spinning, a new role for grandfathers, a wheel for survival. Think about that.

Lendram Spinning Wheel
Ron tries his hand at spinning on the Lendram wheel during his visit to Shady Grove Farm. (Photograph © Naomi Dagen Bloom)

A Wheel Is Born
Ron assembles his new, long-awaited Babe's Spin Wheel in his New York City apartment. (Photograph © Naomi Dagen Bloom)

Give It a Whirl
Early in his spinning career, Ron Bloom experimented with spinning on a handmade drop spindle before testing his skill at a spinning wheel. (Photograph © Naomi Dagen-Bloom)

Knitting

By Jamaica Kincaid

Every knitter has a favorite yarn shop, a place to find the best yarn and patterns, and, most importantly, a place run by a knowledgeable knitter who is always there to help or offer words of encouragement. Jamaica Kincaid captures the spirit of everyone's favorite yarn-shop owner in her short story "Knitting."

Jamaica Kincaid was born Elaine Potter Richardson on the island of Antigua in 1949. Kincaid moved to New York in 1965 and began to write for Ingenue magazine in the early 1970s. It wasn't long before she landed a job at the prestigious New Yorker magazine, where she wrote the "Talk of the Town" column for many years. Kincaid has written a number of novels, including Annie John, Lucy, and Autobiography of My Mother. This story was published in Talk Stories (2001), a collection of Kincaid's New Yorker "Talk of the Town" columns dating from 1974 until 1983.

There is a store called the Country Store & Yarn Shop in the small town of Washington, Connecticut, where one can buy all sorts of materials and instruments used in handicrafts, and especially in knitting. It is perhaps the nicest store in the world, because it is run and owned by perhaps one of the nicest women in the world—a woman named Beatrice Morse Davenport, or Bea to almost everybody who comes into the store. Mrs. Davenport, a gentle-looking, shy, grandmotherly woman, still has the gait of a girl who is afraid she'll be judged too tall, and she peers at objects and people from behind her glasses, her head tilted to one side, in the odd, calm way of someone who makes things with her hands. Mrs. Davenport is quite accomplished in all the needlecrafts, but she is an exceptional knitter, and it is knitting problems, a wish for knitting instruction, and the purchasing of yarns and needles that bring most people to her store. She seems happy to help solve problems, gives instruction free of charge, and offers sound advice on the purchasing of yarns and needles. We visited her in her store the other day, and while she was correcting a mistake made in an enormous afghan by a friend of ours (some stitches dropped four rows down, Mrs. Davenport had told our friend, adding that to unravel the afghan, which was about four yards wide, would mean losing many hours of work) she said these things to us:

"My mother taught me to knit when I was about nine years old. I used to knit all my dolls' clothes. Then I picked up things here and there and I got to be better than my mother. I had to show her how to follow a pattern. I think I made myself a sweater when I was sixteen, and then I just stopped until my first child was coming. Well, you know, if you are going to have a baby you have to make a nice baby sweater. Somebody saw the sweater I made, and wanted one like it, and so I made another sweater, and then somebody

Treasure Chest
Appealing skeins of hand-spun yarn fill a rustic wooden chest in a yarn shop display. (Photograph © Chris Hartlove)

at the New York Exchange for Woman's Work saw it and asked me to knit for them. I knitted things for the Exchange for twelve years. I stopped because I had too many other orders to fill. By that time, I was knitting for designers in New York. I knitted for a woman named Jane von Schreiber. That was in the forties. Few people know who she is today, but in those days she was quite big. Margaret Sommerfeld is another person I knitted for. And somebody named Margaret Macy. I don't remember if I ever saw her. They would just send me a sketch of whatever it was they wanted, and I would make it. I did all this at home while my children were growing up, because I wanted to be with them. When Walt, my son, was ready for college, I began selling yarn. Then, when they were all off at college, I bought a store. My first store was a part of what's now the Washington Food Market, here in Washington.

"Right away, I started selling Irish yarn. I imported the yarns myself from Ireland, because the yarn companies hadn't picked up on Irish yarns yet. People would buy the yarn, but then they would want a pattern to make the yarn into something, so I would just make up a pattern for them. I love to knit so much. If you really want to know, I started to knit for people because my children had all the sweaters they could wear, and by that time I just had to keep knitting, and so I did. The whole thing excites me so much. When I see a new yarn, I think, Oh, I know what should be done with that. It's terrible to be so enthusiastic at my age, isn't it? But it gives me so much satisfaction. I just got a letter from a woman in England telling me about a sweater I had made for her little sister years and years ago. Her sister wore the sweater, and then I guess it was put away, because the sister's four children all wore it at one time or another, and now this woman's son, a cousin of the four children, is wearing it. I had forgotten what it looked like, so she sent me a picture of the little boy wearing it. Now, that's satisfying."

Mrs. Davenport studied the afghan, with all the stitches picked up and correctly in place, and then she looked up and smiled. "There," she said.

—July 12, 1982

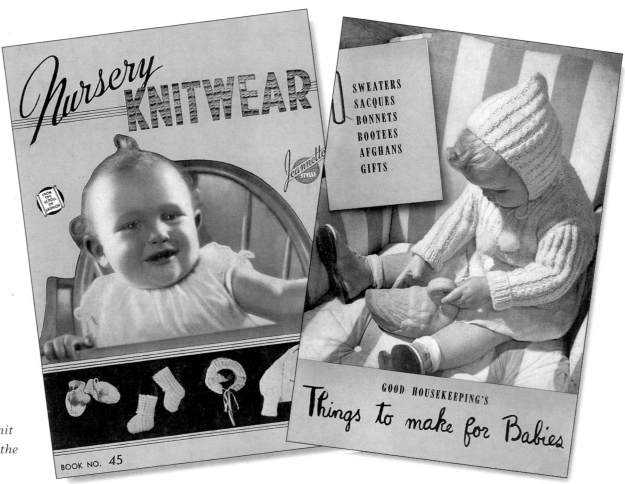

Nursery Knitwear
These pattern books, filled with items to knit for babies, date from the 1940s.

Knitting on the Porch
Sisters while away an afternoon knitting on the family's front porch. (Photograph courtesy of the Library of Congress)

A Bunch of Little Old Ladies

By Kay Dorn

For writer Kay Dorn, the Ladybug Knitting Shop in Dennis, Massachusetts, is a place to catch up with the good friends she's made in her knitting club. Not only do the Ladybug knitters ooh and ahh over the latest completed projects and exchange knitting tips, they talk about what has transpired in their own lives and in the world since the group last met. And, in the true community spirit, every other month the shop's several knitting groups gather for a huge potluck, where knitters talk with old friends and meet new ones.

"A Bunch of Little Old Ladies" was one of two of Kay's essays first published in Knit Lit: Sweaters and Their Stories . . . and Other Writing about Knitting, published by Three Rivers Press in 2002. Kay recently retired from editing a business newspaper. She enjoys knitting for her grandchildren, going for walks, and volunteering at the library.

The flight from California to southern Florida loomed ahead, so I took out my knitting project—a green tunic sweater for my 4-year-old grandson—and began working the cables.

"Amazing," said my seat partner, "how your hands fly. Have you been doing that long?" It doesn't take much to get me talking about knitting and soon I was telling him about our Cape Cod knitting group. Of course, I knew exactly what he was thinking . . . a bunch of little old ladies hobble into a yarn shop, greeted by the blue-haired shop owner who sits in her rocker clicking needles while the group assembles. They sit in a circle, chatting about yesterday's weather.

If he only knew! This group, which meets at the Ladybug Knitting Shop in Dennis, Massachusetts, is not all old and not all ladies; in fact, not all anything. It is a diverse assortment of lives that come together up to four times a week. We suffer along with beginners awkwardly trying to make sense out of those myriad loops of yarn; and we ad-

mire the advanced yarnsmiths who create tiny beaded bags with size 00004 needles. Our knitters include Bob (who makes mittens for his grandkids), realtors, kayakers, antique dealers, homeschooled girls fulfilling their Home Economics requirement, a flight attendant, and (true!) some little old ladies. One of them, Evelyn, came in for knitting lessons at age 82. Now 93, she has her own little ladybug stool to prop her legs on while she knits, perched on a reserved corner seat at our knitting table.

So, far from gossip and small talk, we have an eclectic mix of opinions. We have, for example, decided how Florida should revamp its election process. We've held high-powered conversations on books, retired spouses, hot flashes, health, grandchildren, news events and cooking. And as for that blue-haired knitting-while-she-rocks shop owner, Barbara Prue: the only thing accurate about that description is that she rocks! One day she might be modeling her latest belly-dancing outfit; the next day, she's explaining how she

Knitting for Little Ones
A couple of little old ladies knit baby bonnets in the garden on a pleasant summer afternoon.

applied the henna curlicues to her feet, or talking about the pleasure she gets from her cello lessons.

We're a diverse group and anything but my flight partner's probable profile. But have not a doubt that knitting is a top priority in our lives. Knitting is what draws us together and what we have in common amidst our diversity. Barbara Prue once said, "The most rewarding people to me are the quiet knitters or someone new to the area who hardly says much at first, but seems to soak it all up. They seem to gain the most from the companionship and new friendships." It is these friendships, which now go well beyond the knitting table that we treasure so much.

These ties have resulted in people launching adventures they never would have tried alone. They've given strength to the newly bereaved—in fact, our group is often the first outing they tackle as they put their lives back together. We cry for each other at times like these; and we smile with joy when one of us passes around photos of a new baby and chooses yarn for the requisite blankie. Some members of our group have been attending for years; others have just joined and marvel at the closeness of these friends. Some come, solve their knitting problem and leave. Others join us, feel the camaraderie and stay.

Why? Besides a love of knitting, what holds us together? One clue is our instructor, and friend, Nancy Downy. "Special" says it all about Nancy. When she is not busy at her gardener and caretaker jobs, she oversees our knitting groups. She exclaims joyfully at each finished project, and patiently explains, sometimes for the fifth time, how to execute a new stitch. She graciously rips out mistakes, when we cannot bear to do it ourselves, and repairs the damage. We can take on projects that are more complicated or creative than we tackle on our own because we know we can always call, "Nancy, help!" And each day when we leave the Ladybug Shop, we know something new—maybe a different way to cast on or a better way of increasing—all because of Nancy.

Do we need another reason for giving up a trip to the beach or lunch with a friend for an hour in the shop? We're charmed by the rainbow of colors and textures lurking temptingly on the Ladybug's shelves. One knitter brings in the mint-green fuzzy jacket that she's knitting for her granddaughter—and a dozen others love it. "I must make that," each cries, and Barbara traipses up her circular stairway to the storage room and carries down more of that de-licious yarn. We also contribute our skills as a group. One year we all made hats and mittens for the homeless; another year we made afghans for Project Linus, to be distributed to terminally ill children.

Our once-a-month birthday cakes have evolved into an every-other-month supper of hors d'oeuvres and dessert. We love meeting the knitters who attend groups on different days than we do, and we get to try delicious new foods and swap recipes. We are grateful for Nancy and Barbara and all those at Ladybug who create this way of life for us—who make the challenge of taking up our needles such a pleasure. They provide the opportunity to meet new friends, keep our minds alert and expand our knitting skills.

So much for little old ladies... I thought about the Ladybug as I worked on my cables, and I smiled to myself.

Knitted Teacups, 1993
Debbie New designed these wonderful life-size teacups using different stitch patterns that allow the cups to stand on their own, without stiffening the yarn. (Photograph by Brian Céré of Dumont Group Photography, Kitchener, Ont.)

Knitting Hands
A knitter's hands move in a steady rhythm as she works a sweater pattern in the round. (Photograph © Chris Hartlove)

Close-Knit Family
Three sisters gather circa 1880 to knit, sew, and tat while they catch up on one another's lives and the news around town. (Photograph courtesy of the Minnesota Historical Society)

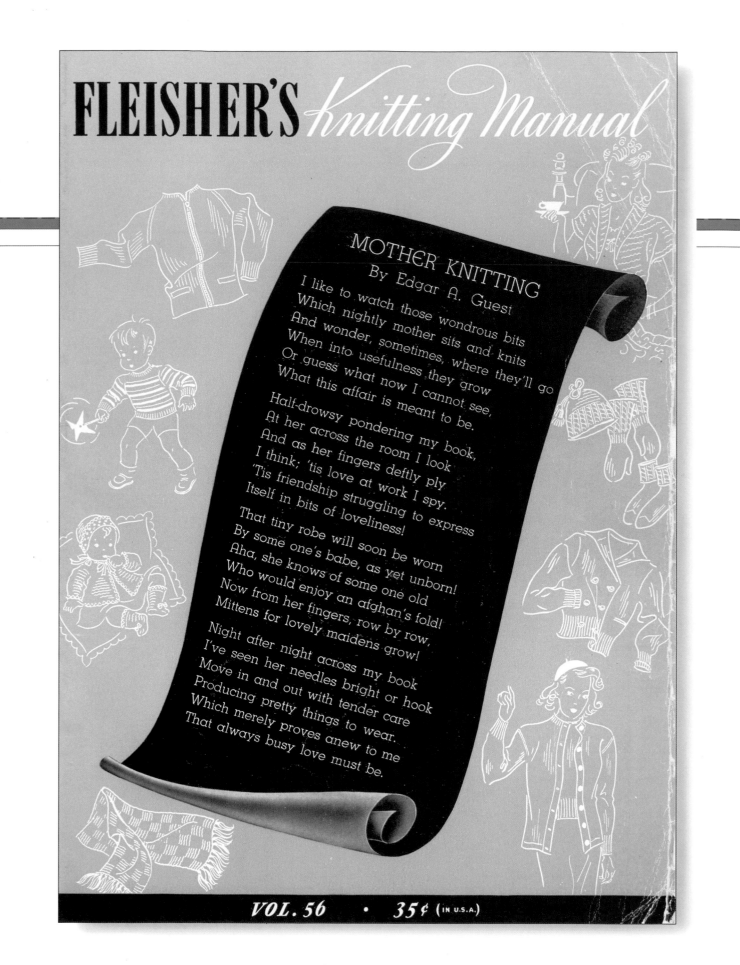

FLEISHER'S *Knitting Manual*

MOTHER KNITTING
By Edgar A. Guest

I like to watch those wondrous bits
Which nightly mother sits and knits
And wonder, sometimes, where they'll go
When into usefulness they grow
Or guess what now I cannot see,
What this affair is meant to be.

Half-drowsy pondering my book,
At her across the room I look
And as her fingers deftly ply
I think; 'tis love at work I spy.
'Tis friendship struggling to express
Itself in bits of loveliness!

That tiny robe will soon be worn
By some one's babe, as yet unborn!
Aha, she knows of some one old
Who would enjoy an afghan's fold!
Now from her fingers, row by row,
Mittens for lovely maidens grow!

Night after night across my book
I've seen her needles bright or hook
Move in and out with tender care
Producing pretty things to wear.
Which merely proves anew to me
That always busy love must be.

CHAPTER 3

HANDKNIT WITH LOVE

CONSIDER A GRANDMOTHER KNITTING A SWEATER FOR A GRANDCHILD JUST COMING INTO THE WORLD. INTO THE STITCHES FOR THAT SWEATER GO ALL THE GRANDMOTHER'S PRAYERS FOR SAFE DELIVERY, ALL OF HER GOOD FEELINGS ABOUT THE CHILD AND ITS PARENTS. THE WORK ITSELF IS A PRAYER FOR THE SAFETY AND WELL-BEING OF MOTHER AND CHILD, A LABOR OF LOVE, A RITUAL WELCOMING OF NEW LIFE INSIDE THE EXTENDED FAMILY OR TRIBE.

—*Susan Gordon Lydon, from Knitting: History, Fashion, and Great Knitting Yarns, 2000*

Inevitably, anyone who picks up a pair of knitting needles and yarn will be entranced by the notion of knitting the most perfect gift for a family member, close friend, or loved one. What could be more thoughtful, more heartfelt than a sweater, cap, scarf, mittens, or afghan knit by hand? Most knitters delve into the creation of each new gift knowing it can be a monumental task. There is so much to consider—selecting just the right project, finding the perfect color, the most suitable yarn, and, perhaps most importantly, finishing the project on time—all the while hoping the recipient will like the gift when it is finished. Despite all of these challenges, knitters continue to defy all odds and knit warm gifts for loved ones, gifts that are surely treasured, even those that spend more time in the recipient's dresser than on his or her back.

"Mother Knitting"
In addition to the patterns inside, Fleischer's Knitting Manual from 1939 came with an extra special bonus: a quaint poem by Edgar A. Guest about the lovely gifts his mother knits for friends and relatives.

Handknit Sweater
There's nothing more beautiful or heartfelt than the gift of a handknit sweater. (Photograph © Chris Hartlove)

BOOK NO. 240

10¢

Men's Sweaters

Chadwick's
RED ♥ HEART
Wools

Two Sweaters for My Father

By Perri Klass

As a young girl, author Perri Klass promised to knit a sweater for her father. In this essay, a shorter version of which appeared in the winter 2002 issue of Knitter's magazine, Klass relates each step of the project in heartwarming detail. Perri Klass is a pediatrician in Boston, and medical director of the Reach Out and Read National Center. She is the author of several books, including The Mystery of Breathing and Love and Modern Medicine. Klass is a regular columnist for Knitter's magazine.

I was very young when I made the first one, probably in seventh or eighth grade. I had done a little knitting and a little crocheting—I had a scarf or two to my name. I used to work on them in the evenings while my father read aloud.

He read to us at night all through my childhood—ambitious lengthy projects (we got all the way through *The Hobbit* and the entire trilogy of *The Lord of the Rings*, back in the late 1960s when it was a fixture on college campuses; I would walk with him across the campus of Columbia University, where he taught, and see students carrying volumes of Tolkien, or wearing "Frodo Lives" buttons, and I would feel a grade-school child's sense of pride at being on the inside). He read us volumes of P. G. Wodehouse, doing the British accents with tremendous enthusiasm, and it is still his voice that I hear when I read Wodehouse. Even as I grew into a somewhat difficult preadolescent, I wanted to be part of those evenings on the couch, along with my younger brother—but I was twitchy, prone to playing with my hair or pulling at stray threads on my clothing, and the knitting was a happy compromise to keep my hands busy without driving everyone else crazy. So I had made my endless scarves, and it was time to take on a new challenge; I would make my father a sweater.

Now, Papa was fairly conservative when it came to clothing. No one ever succeeded, not even my mother, in choosing a Father's Day tie for him that he was willing to wear, no matter how conservatively we chose. He liked beautiful things, but they were conservative beautiful things—a Harris Tweed jacket, a solid-color Shetland wool pullover bought on a trip to Scotland. He wore button-down shirts, with those careful, safe, striped or solid ties that he chose for himself. No eccentricity, no idiosyncrasy; he dressed like the professor he was. He was not, in short, a man you could easily imagine wearing a middle school kid's first attempt at a handmade sweater.

But my father had great faith. He believed that his children could do anything. When I played the viola, Papa came to recitals and imagined me going on to a career in music (it probably helped that he was himself completely tone-deaf, and therefore unable to hear how ill-suited I, his tone-deaf daughter, was to an instrument where ear matters so much). When I wrote stories, he imagined me going on to publication and success and literary immortality. And when he saw me sitting there working with wool, he thought I could make him a sweater, and a sweater he would be able to wear. And I agreed. I loved the feeling of knitting and

"Men's Sweaters"
The "Men's Sweaters" pattern book, published by Chadwick's Red Heart Wools in 1947, offers ten sweaters, from turtlenecks to short-sleeve tees, in a wide range of styles, providing plenty of ideas to the young knitter who's considering knitting a sweater for a loved one.

crocheting, loved how it helped me sit still and listen, and if Papa wanted a sweater, I was sure it was just a matter of choosing the yarn. And the yarn he chose, of course, was conservative: dark gray 100 percent wool, wound in those giant dog-biscuit shaped skeins, a bulge at either end, a center wrapped in shiny black paper. With great importance, I carried home a sack full of skeins, dye lot carefully matched (I think there was a warning on that shiny black label about buying enough wool from the same dye lot to complete your project, and Papa, who began worrying the minute the gas gauge on his car dipped below half full, certainly didn't want me to take any risks. I bought enough wool and more than enough: this was going to be a *major* sweater.)

You know how there are certain projects on which you look back wondering what possessed you? Where you can't understand how this could ever EVER have seemed like a good—or even plausible—idea, and you wonder why on earth you didn't see that before you put in all this work? Well, that is how I feel about my decision to make my father's cardigan sweater by single crochet. I think there must have been a particular pattern in a little booklet of sweaters to knit and crochet, and I remember a black and white photo of a gentleman in an appropriately conservative cardigan, rather small and grainy, but promising a highly suitable garment. I took one look and hitched my wagon to that particular vision, and I started to crochet for all I was worth. I have always been a tight knitter—and crocheter—and I worked with a small hook. The result was a fabric with real, how would you say, body, to it. A material that stood up on its own and claimed its territory. I think it would probably have come in handy on an ill-fated Polar expedition—surely it would have kept out the arctic chill, and in a pinch, perhaps you could have stretched the sweater between two poles and hitched it directly to the sled dogs as a travois to carry a badly frostbitten comrade. As this dense grey matter took form under my fingers, I swelled with pride, and, in my enthusiasm, working my way through skein after skein, I made the sweater longer and longer. I had never really tried to follow a pattern before, never shaped sleeves or armholes, but I muddled along, and learned a certain amount on the first side that I was able to apply to the second—which was, consequently, a different shape. I did manage to get the sleeves of roughly equal length, but again, in

my pride and enthusiasm, I made them very long indeed.

So there you have it. I had created a longer-than-waist-length jacket that looked rather like it was made out of stiff, grey corrugated cardboard with high, tight armholes, one set differently from the other, and sleeves long enough for an orangutan. It was, without question, a cardigan sweater, of a kind. Did I mention that I had also taught myself to make buttonholes, and that the front band of the sweater clearly reflected my progress in this direction? The second buttonhole was better than the first, and the seventh was really quite respectable.

Why didn't I rip out and redo? Well, I've never been very good about doing that; when it comes to the actual knitting (or crocheting), I am tight and compulsive, but I have this fatal tendency to believe that errors in pattern and shaping will all miraculously stretch into place—or at least into invisibility—when the whole project is put together.

My lap was now blanketed in sweater as I sat on the couch and listened to my father read aloud. Everyone was impressed as the sweater grew, I assumed—my younger brother over on the other end of the couch, my mother, passing through the living room, and most of all, my father. I had created something, well, substantial. Something massive. A monument of a sweater.

I bought fancy silver buttons and sewed them on, and presented my father with his sweater. And god bless him, I do believe he wore it occasionally—I mean, not out of the house (there was no pressing Polar expedition) or where other people might see him, but he did wear it. And that was the first sweater I ever made for anyone—and the first and last crocheted garment I ever made. I went back to knitting scarves on the living room couch, putting down the crochet hook with some relief—my right hand was getting tired.

Well, thirty or so years went by, and I did a lot of knitting. I learned to make sweaters that fit—or at least, to knit for children and aim a little large, and know that eventually the child's growth trajectory would intersect the sweater size. I got much better at little details like appropriate sleeve length, shoulder shaping, and even buttonholes (though I still often find that the last buttonhole on a sweater looks nicer than the first—and I still don't always rip out and redo when I should). A few years ago, I offered to knit my father another sweater, thinking, in part, of that

Minerva Knitting Manual
Knitting swatches in a variety of color and stitch patterns wave like flags on the cover of this 1951 pattern book, which is filled with knitting ideas for the entire family.

What Could Be Better Than a Cardigan?
Two patterns from the summer 1944 issue of the McCall's Needlework Knitting and Crocheting *magazine sing the praises of the ever-versatile cardigan, one made for a man, the other designed for a woman.*

early effort, and of the possibility of setting the balance right by making him something soft and properly shaped out of expensive luxurious yarn.

Papa was enthusiastic, of course. Even when his children were grown up, he still believed we could do anything. His sympathetic imagination followed us along every bend of the career path and into every new adventure, always assuming we had only to decide how to bestow our talents, and the world was ours. If I had wanted to be a molecular geneticist, I would be a molecular geneticist. If I had wanted to be surgeon general, I would be surgeon general. So if I wanted to knit him a sweater, the masterpiece would soon be keeping him warm. One weekend when my parents came up to Cambridge, we went to the yarn store, and after tremendous deliberation, Papa found a pattern he liked, for an intricately patterned vest, knit fair isle style in subtle muted colors. Could I knit that, he asked, in wonder at my talents. And of course I said of course, never mind that it was a much finer gauge than I usually knit, never mind that the pattern was singularly ill-suited for the kind of knitting-in-meetings that I usually do. We bought the pattern and the wool and the needles, and I took them home, where they joined a procession of intended projects, a queue of good intentions and impulsive yarn purchases long enough to guide me through the next thirty years, if not longer. Now, I do pick up these projects—or some of them—and I do complete one every now and then, though it's also true that at times I shamelessly bypass this patient waiting group of dear old friends to run off with a new enthusiasm, some exceptionally snazzy yarn or some wildly appealing pattern which has suddenly jumped the line.

But what I'm trying to say here is, I never made Papa that vest. I intended to make it some day, I think—some day when there was a moment for careful patterned knitting. I had the wool carefully put away with notes on Papa's measurements, taken from a favorite vest of his. But I never unpacked the wool and the pattern and the measurements, never made a swatch, never cast on for that vest.

My father died, very suddenly and unexpectedly, in April of 2001. He was healthy, as far as anybody knew, and

Lion Brand Yarn
A late-1940s advertisement for Lion Brand Cashmere yarn features a beautifully knit, cabled men's vest.

enjoying his retirement, after forty years of college teaching—he was a cultural anthropologist who studied South Asia and religion and the Caribbean. He had recently published a book and was in the middle of writing two others. He developed a pain in his chest one day, while he and my mother were eating lunch, and then, just like that, he died.

I found myself making lists, sometimes, in the months after his death, of what I regretted most—specific things I had never said, or done, or asked while my father was alive. I made myself balance those lists by itemizing the things I was particularly glad I had said or done—conversations I had had with my father, trips we'd taken, meals we'd eaten.

And I thought about that vest that I never made for Papa. To be honest, it wasn't one of my regrets—maybe I knew, even in the worst of my grief, that that vest was probably unrealistic—that it wasn't really my kind of knitting, that I would have been very unlikely to finish it, even if I had started it. Or maybe I suspected that even if I had started it and finished it, it would never have attained the right fit, the correct and conservative proportions which would have let my father wear it without feeling self-conscious. Or maybe I thought the vest always had more value as a promise to be fulfilled than it could have had as a garment.

I think now about my father and those two sweaters. I have kids of my own, and I think I finally understand both how much you might value a completely unwearable garment which represents the pride and love and effort of your child—and also how you might be able to continue believing, thirty years later, in that same child's ability to make something complicated, perfect, and beautiful. And also, I guess, about the ways that in family life, errors in pattern and shaping really *can* stretch miraculously into place when the whole project is put together.

I haven't seen that gray sweater in decades. When I started thinking about writing this essay, I called my mother and asked her to look through my father's clothing for the sweater, so she could describe it to me and confirm my memory. It took my mother a while to find it, because the gray sweater wasn't where she had thought it would be—in the hall closet where she and my father kept the jackets and clothing they rarely wore. I was sure my father had kept it, perhaps folded away in a box of other arts and crafts projects from my childhood, ceramic ashtrays and hand-drawn wall calendars treasured for their sentimental value. But my parents had sold their house after all the children were grown, and had moved to an apartment. They had thrown away an awful lot of accumulated junk, and put many such boxes in storage. My mother had no very clear memory of the sweater, now more than thirty years old, which she had, of course, not seen my father wearing on a daily basis—or indeed ever. But she kept looking, and finally she called me.

"Guess where I found it?" she said. "It was put away in the bedroom closet—where Papa kept all his very best clothes."

Knitting Needles by Candlelight
A collection of wooden needles topped with hand-carved folk characters fill a colorful vase. (Photograph © Chris Hartlove)

fascinating

Toppers

Knitter's Jitters: How I Stitched My Way to Wedding-Day Bliss

By Margret Aldrich

It has always been a tradition for the bride to give gifts to her bridesmaids as a way of showing her appreciation for their friendship and support over the years. In this essay, writer Margret Aldrich goes above and beyond the call of duty by handknitting each of her attendants a hat. Margret and her new husband live in Princeton, New Jersey, where she is the intellectual property associate at Princeton University Press. She also works as a freelance writer and is the editor of three anthologies, This Old Quilt, Every Quilt Tells a Story, *and coeditor of* This Old Guitar, *all from Voyageur Press.*

A thousand and one things are involved in planning a wedding. There are dresses to try on, guests to invite, and vows to write. There are menus to plan, songs to select, and flowers to choose. There are cakes to taste, ministers to meet, manicures to get, and—in my case—hats to knit.

Although I didn't go overboard and knit my own flowing wedding gown or a three-piece suit for the groom-to-be, I did want to show my bridesmaids how much I appreciated their friendship and support by making them each a heartfelt, handmade gift. I had taken only one knitting class the previous winter, and my bevy of completed items consisted of a scarf (not long enough) and two hats (one too big, one too small). Needless to say, my skills were limited. Out of practicality, I decided to knit hats for my bridesmaids—they seemed to stitch up a bit more quickly, and if one of the women happened to have a bad hair day on the afternoon of the nuptials, she could always stuff her unruly locks into her new stocking cap. Four months before the wedding, the project began.

I should mention that there were five bridesmaids. That may seem excessive, but each of them was irreplaceable—my sister, my future sister-in-law, my oldest friend, and my two closest girlfriends and roommates from college. Five hats in four months gave me three weeks per hat, which seemed like plenty of time, even if I was working a full-time job, finishing up my master's degree, and co-planning a wedding.

With that now-familiar feeling of anticipation and exhilaration that bubbles up when I go to the yarn shop with a project in mind, I went to my favorite, local knitting-supply store. The variegated yarn I selected was dyed with muted tones of coral, green, lilac, and white, making

Fascinating Toppers
This 1944 pattern book, filled with hats and scarves to knit and crochet, claims to be a woman's "headquarters" for glamour.

A Little Help from My Friends
A young woman knits a scarf while her friends gather around, clowning for the camera in this vintage photograph from the early 1900s.

it unnecessary to work in a pattern with a contrasting color—that alone would save me countless, precious hours. I snatched up an armful of the woolen skeins, settled up at the cash register, and headed home to start hat number one.

Knitting that first hat was like therapy. As each stitch fell off the smooth, straight, wooden needles, a little bit of tension fell away from my neck and shoulders. Knitting allowed me to sit and reflect, listen to music or the TV, or even talk with a friend—as long as I wasn't doing something too complicated, like increasing or decreasing (I lose track of my stitch counts embarrassingly easily). Hat number one was completed ahead of schedule and, although it was rather small for my oddly large skull, I knew it would fit a normal-sized head just fine.

Stitching the second hat was equally pleasurable. I sat on the couch with my feet up on the coffee table and worked in stockinette—knitting one row and purling the next. I was having such a good time and was feeling so relaxed, I tried to convince my fiancé, Gary, that he should take up knitting. As someone who constantly twirls his hair, twists his beard, or plays with my ponytail, I was sure he'd be a natural. He decided to leave the knitting to me. Hat number two took longer to finish than the first one, but as I stitched up the seam and wove in the yarn end, I was still on schedule.

Hat number three prompted an interesting conversation with my coworker and fellow knitter, Kari: Is it possible to knit and drive at the same time? She claimed to have seen a woman knitting as she motored her car down Interstate 94. Although Kari didn't condone this practice, it did make us muse over all of the rows we could complete on our thirty-five-minute commute. Time is what I needed. I was finding it harder and harder to fit knitting into my day and considered the fact that I may have bitten off more than I could chew.

As I started hat number four, I began to wonder if any of the bridesmaids were expendable. This contemplation quickly passed, of course, and I thought with great relief about the upcoming trip to Hawaii that Gary and I were about to take. He needed to attend a conference there, so we had decided to make it a kind of pre-wedding honeymoon. Although I was looking forward to mai-tais and the music of steel guitars, I was also excited about the nine-hour plane ride—plenty of time to get some work done on the bridesmaids' hats. Between a much-needed nap and the in-flight movie, however, I didn't complete a single stitch on hat number four while we were en route to Honolulu. That week, the hat went with us to Waikiki Beach, where I did a row or two, and drove with us to the North Shore of Oahu, where I completed another few rows as we watched surfers tackle the best waves on the island. Mostly, the hat sat in my suitcase in the hotel room. On our flight back to the mainland, I tried to make up for lost time, knitting furiously as Gary snoozed beside me. Twenty minutes before we touched down, hat number four was done, its stitches smelling vaguely of suntan lotion.

With less than a month left before our big day, every moment seemed to be filled with appointments, fittings, or other wedding-related activities. The weeks slipped by, and the only headway on hat number five was a line of cast-on stitches and two lonely rows. Kari offered to serve as my surrogate knitter and finish up that last hat, but because the point of giving these silly gifts to my bridesmaids was that I wanted them each to have something made by me with love, I was determined to complete the final hat myself. I packed it away in my suitcase and got ready to make the trek to my parents' farm in Iowa, where I would stay the week before the wedding.

Those seven days were occupied with family get-togethers and last-minute preparations. I picked up my needles every now and then, but progress was slow. The rehearsal dinner was slated for Friday night, and I wanted to be sure all five hats were finished by then, so I could give them to my bridesmaids after the meal. That meant hat number five had to be complete by Thursday night—Friday was completely booked with activities.

Worse than wedding-day jitters, I had knitter's jitters—that sinking feeling that comes with the realization that you might not get your project done before a major deadline, like Christmas morning or your husband's birthday. When Thursday rolled around, my jitters were at their peak. I woke up and knit in my pajamas until the shower was free. Then, I knit some more while my breakfast got cold. I knit in the passenger seat of my sister's car on our way to her pedicure appointment at Nikki's Nails. I pulled up a chair next to her to talk and knit as she was buffed, painted, and moisturized. On the way home, as my needles clicked against each other, she asked if I were getting tired of knitting. "It relaxes me," I said as my fingers started to cramp.

After dinner and the three hours we spent figuring out the seating arrangement for the reception, I sat down to continue working on hat number five, knitter's jitters escalating to an alarming level. One by one my family members went to bed. One by one my stitches multiplied. By midnight, I had developed the affliction knitters everywhere are familiar with—that burning ache centered between the shoulder blades, right where you can't quite reach to rub it out. But at 2 A.M., that hat was done. The stitching was impeccable, the seam straight, and the decreases swirled into a star at the cap's summit. I climbed the stairs to my old room and fell into bed without a single jitter or worry in my head.

Intricate Stitch Pattern
Winding the working yarn around her forefinger, a knitter stitches her way through an intricate stitch pattern in the late afternoon light. (Photograph © Chris Hartlove)

The next day was full of excitement and energy. Gary arrived and gift wrapped the hats for me, as I finished writing out a few last place-cards. Our friends and family began showing up in pairs and quartets, offering their help to fix any final details. My aunt threw a bridal luncheon for me and my bridesmaids, and then we all headed to the church for the rehearsal. After we figured out the logistics of the ceremony and had dinner and drinks at a local restaurant, I passed out the gifts to my bridesmaids. They tore off the wrapping paper and pulled out their hats, which had been such an intimate part of my life for the last four months, worrying with me, traveling with me, staying up late with me, and ultimately calming me as I prepared for this monumental weekend. The women didn't seem to notice the hats' imperfections or simple pattern as they modeled them for the rest of our friends and family and remarked on the thoughtfulness of handmade gifts—even though they considered me crazy for devoting the hours it took to finish them. My sister laughed, realizing why I had been knitting so intently and intensely the day before. I beamed as I thought about each of my bridesmaids remembering this night whenever they put on one of those damn hats.

Then came the question that all of the ladies were thinking: "Um, are we supposed to wear these the day of the wedding?" Lucky for them, the stress of the last several months hadn't quite pushed me over the edge, and I assured them that they would be walking down the aisle sans hats. It was August, after all. Perhaps a February wedding would have been a different story.

Our wedding was unforgettable. The flowers were beautiful, the cake delicious, the guests happy, and I only tripped on my dress once. We couldn't have asked for a more perfect day. There is a small part of me, however, that's glad it's over, I must admit. Now I can finally, truly relax. All of the planning that went into our big event, all of the jitters, and all of the knitting are over.

Except that Traci, one of our readers during the ceremony, is having a baby in less than two weeks . . . Jen, my personal attendant, is due a month after that . . . two of Gary's stepsisters are also in the family way . . . and when I was flipping through a knitting magazine today, I saw a perfect pattern for the sweetest, little baby hat. . . .

Multitasking
Ralph Pallen Coleman's colorfully illustrated cover for the March 1935 issue of Needlecraft: The Home Arts Magazine *urges knitters not to knit while behind the wheel, no matter how much they're certain to accomplish on that lengthy road trip.*

Crowning Glories
In the 1940s, hat pins, decorative hair combs, and other flourishes were favorite ways to top off a hat with style.

Fun in the Sun
What could be better than knitting or crocheting a few rows on your latest project while soaking up a few rays?

Amelia

By Melanie Falick

y by Melanie Falick, a woman and a teenager knit together on a summer after-
lick is the author of Weekend Knitting published in 2003 by Stewart, Tabori &
tting published in 1998 by Artisan, and Knitting in America published in 1996 by
he coauthor of Knitting for Baby, published in 2002 by Stewart, Tabori & Chang.

y herself most of the summer in a
ie hill. Upstairs, in what for a long
study, I would see her writing and
ich there was nearly always a vase
i she sometimes hosted guests for
stayed alone in her house, a house
mone family for as long as anyone
er. She awoke early—I knew that be-
sipping tea on her porch as the sun
late, often knitting until well past
my mother, who walked late at night,

rived for her first summer, I was im-
For so long, the Simone family had
rented out the house for months—even years—at a time, leaving the upkeep of it to a sturdy, old French woman named
Lucille Lavolle. Madame Lavolle, as she referred to herself

when calling for services around town, barely revealed a
word about the house or the Simone family to anyone, which
made them seem even more mysterious to me.

There wasn't a lot to do in our town, so until I was old
enough to drive away I would spend many summer days at
the riverbank. I would walk along the river and peer up to
Amelia's porch and into her windows. She was pretty and
didn't look very old—I guessed she was about the same age
as my mother—and I couldn't imagine why she came to our
town. I thought she might be a widow.

Amelia didn't have a garden of her own, so every Saturday morning she would put on a sleeveless green cotton
dress—the type of house dress I remembered my grandmother wearing—and ride her old, squeaky bike to the
farmer's market at the pier to buy fruits, vegetables, flowers, and bread. When she was finished, she would strap her
purchases into the wire baskets on the back of her bike and

Tiffany Vest
Vibrant, asymmetrical sunflowers make up the majority of Debbie New's almost knee-length Tiffany Vest. (Photograph ©
Sandy Nicholson Photography)

ride home. During my last summer in town—when I was seventeen—I actually got to know Amelia a little bit. In the spring I had started working at the bakery and on Saturdays it was my job to sell bread from the back of an old pickup truck at the market. Each time I saw Amelia, she would ask me if any of the breads were still warm and then would buy whichever one I pointed out unless it was raisin bread, which she consistently declined. Before putting the loaf in her bag, she would rip off a piece to eat right there, which always seemed exotic to me.

One day, after chewing some warm sourdough bread, Amelia surprised me and asked a question. "Do you know if there is a knitting shop nearby?" she said. I was taken aback—as Amelia had never before spoken to me about anything except the bread. It took me a moment to comprehend her words.

"No, I don't," I answered finally. But I smiled because when I looked at her, I realized that I wanted to know her, I needed to know someone in this town who didn't know me or my family.

"That's too bad," Amelia answered. "I broke one of my needles last night."

I don't know where I got the nerve, as I was usually very shy, but I told her I could see if my mom, who used to knit, had an extra needle she could borrow. "I could drop it off at your house later," I told her. "What size?"

"Size six, double-pointed," she answered. "I live at the top of the hill, in the blue house overlooking the river. My name is Amelia."

"Yes, I know. I'm Zan."

I watched Amelia move to the flower vendor and then pack her bike and ride away. She seemed so calm and comfortable. I had offered to go out of my way for her and she responded politely, yet she didn't get nervous or ask me if it was too much trouble and offer me a way out of the favor the way my mom—and most of the women I knew—would do. They always apologized for being "any trouble," even when they weren't any trouble at all.

Later that afternoon, when I knocked on Amelia's door with the needles I had dug out of the back of my mom's closet, I was disappointed to find there was no answer. As the door was unlocked, I pushed it gently and called out a few times to see if I might find her.

"I'll be right down," Amelia called from somewhere upstairs. For what felt like a long time but was probably only about five minutes, Amelia stayed upstairs and I wandered

A Greater Measure of Knitting Pleasure
Smart, sporty styles for women grace the pages of a pattern book published by Bear Brand and Bucilla Yarns in 1940.

Bernat's Handknit Classics
A beautifully stitched short-sleeved cardigan in sizes for mother and daughter are featured on the cover of this pattern booklet from 1945.

A Bed of Sweaters
Stacks of stunning Norwegian sweaters designed by Solveig Hisdal make a most comfortable nest for a sleepy cat. (Photograph © Solveig Hisdal)

around her living room, which had big windows with river views on two sides. There wasn't much furniture but there was a wooden table full of photos of a family, apparently her family. This, of course, surprised me because I always assumed she lived alone all year, not just in the summer. There were pictures of Amelia with a bearded man, a girl with curly light-brown hair just like hers, and a few different dogs. They looked happy. Taped to the wall above the photos was a piece of old newspaper on which someone had written in large black letters, "Let us be poised, and wise, and our own today—Ralph Waldo Emerson." On another wall and hanging from some rafters on the ceiling were what looked like more than a hundred long, skinny strips of knitting. Some were fringed or had bells attached; some were multicolored; some had colorful patterns in them; some were plain.

I was examining the knitting when Amelia came down the steps wearing paint-splattered overalls, a tank top, and flip-flops, her long hair wet and twisted in a knot. "I've been making those knitted garlands for years," Amelia said. "Knitting helps me to write."

"You're a writer?" I asked.

"I try," she replied.

Amelia didn't explain herself any further and I didn't feel comfortable asking more, so I began to fumble through my backpack to find my mom's needles. When I dropped one and bent down to pick it up, I saw a large pink duffel bag with clothes packed in it tucked next to a chair.

"Here are the needles," I said, wanting to know why she had a duffel bag packed but not asking.

"Thank you. I am finishing a sweater for my daughter. She is leaving for college and I want her to have something special from me."

"Where is your daughter now?" I blurted out and immediately regretted. I hardly knew Amelia and felt I shouldn't be asking her a personal question. But Amelia didn't seem to mind.

"My daughter is at home with her father, my husband. I come here every summer because I need some time alone."

"Don't they like it here?" I asked.

"They like it here very much. But I don't want them to come. I haven't really wanted anyone in my family here."

Amelia had by now sat down on a worn-out yellowish armchair in the corner and was looking out the window toward the river.

"Do you know how to knit?" she asked. "Would you like to work on a garland?"

I told her I hadn't knitted in years but I would try.

"There are a few garlands started under the table," she said, pointing toward a huge, old wooden bowl beneath the table with the photos.

In the bowl were four strips on needles and many small balls of yarn, which I assumed were leftovers from other projects. I chose a fuzzy light blue strip that was only about six inches long. When I sat down in another armchair near Amelia's, this one covered with a striped cotton blanket, I saw that she had pulled out the sweater for her daughter, a brown pullover with stitches that looked like cobwebs around the neck. Amelia explained that it was handspun cashmere. I touched the sweater, which was missing half a sleeve but was otherwise complete. It was softer than any piece of clothing I had ever felt before.

I needed some help getting started on my garland but quickly my fingers remembered what my mother had taught me long ago, before my father had left us and she became too sad to do most everything. Amelia and I talked on and off while we knitted. I told her that I had just finished high school, that I had just broken up with my boyfriend, that my real name was Suzanne, which I hated, but everyone called me Zan, which I preferred. I told her I was leaving for college in a few weeks. I didn't tell her my aunt had picked up my mother in February and taken her to live with

Hero Standard Is My Choice!
A 1948 advertisement for Hero Standard knitting needles promises that knitters will be satisfied with the "velvet smooth plastic and snowflake light aluminum" needles, available in pastel colors, in straight or circular.

her, that I would be packing up everything in the house so that my aunt could come back and put the house up for sale once I was gone. I didn't tell her that I had been pregnant, that I had planned to have an abortion but had had a miscarriage before the appointment.

And Amelia started to tell me why she stayed in the house alone.

"I realized when my daughter was still very young that I resented her and her father," she began. "I loved them but I wasn't happy. I needed time to myself. I just couldn't be like the other mothers; I couldn't pretend it was okay. So I started coming here so I could. . . . " Amelia laughed a little, ". . . renew myself."

When Amelia spoke of the other mothers, I knew she wasn't referring to my mother, the depressed kind who barely ventured out of her house. She was referring to the mothers who signed up their kids for swim classes and gymnastics, who got dressed every morning and never forgot to make dinner. She was talking about the mother I had always wished for. But something Amelia said caught me off-guard—"I just couldn't be like the other mothers. I couldn't pretend it was okay."

"You don't think most mothers are happy?" I asked and put down my knitting.

Amelia looked at me warmly, seeing the confusion in my eyes, and said quietly, "I think all mothers love their children. And some mothers are happy."

Amelia and I didn't talk for quite awhile after this. We both knitted. She worked around and around down the sleeve. And my garland grew. It was getting late—I could see the sun setting. I felt like I should leave but I didn't. And she didn't ask me to leave. I kept thinking about my mother and the baby I was afraid to have and how much I

liked Amelia and was also disappointed by her. She wasn't sick like my mother but she abandoned her daughter every summer. Yet there she was knitting for her daughter the most beautiful sweater I had ever seen.

Amelia broke our silence and asked, "Do you want to hang up your garland here or take it home?"

I wanted to hang it up with Amelia's, to feel like I was part of this house, to be sure Amelia remembered me. It had grown to nearly five feet long, so I asked her to bind off the stitches for me. She bound off the first few, reminding me how to do it myself, and handed the knitting back to me so she could fish a hook out of a drawer at the table. I held a chair while she stood on it and suspended my garland from the ceiling.

When she finished, Amelia stepped down off the chair and stood next to me. "Zan, I know about your mother," she said. "My Aunt Lucille told me this afternoon." She took a deep breath. "We all try to cope. Some people think I'm crazy, that I'm a bad mother, because I leave every summer, because I knit useless pieces of knitting and hang them from the ceiling."

"I know," I said, not really knowing anything at all but needing to say something, to do something to hold back the tears. I looked away from Amelia, started fingering another garland, one with stripes in lots of colors, with strands of yarn hanging down at every place where the colors changed. I could feel the muscles around my mouth twitching. I was biting my lower lip. I looked out the window at the lights flickering on in the houses along the other side of the river. After a few deep breaths, I gathered up my courage and asked, "May I knit another garland?"

"Yes," she answered.

I felt relieved.

Still Life with Needles
A warm tranquil corner of master knitter Kristin Nicholas's home, decorated with knitting odds and ends, begs passersby to pick up a ball of yarn and a pair of needles and cast on. (Photograph © Chris Hartlove)

The Afghan

By Amy Votava

Although the following short story is about a young woman who doesn't knit, she and her husband are very grateful to the Cambridge Church knitting group for their thoughtful gift in a time of need. Author Amy Votava is a fiction writer who lives in Minneapolis, Minnesota, with her husband, David, and her daughter, Olivia. She is currently working on her M.F.A. in creative writing at Hamline University. Knitting with her knitting group is one of Amy's favorite ways to take a break from her studies.

Anika has never been the crafty sort; she's never in her life picked up a knitting needle, has never pumped her foot on the pedal of a sewing machine, and she has only threaded a sewing needle twice in her life. She has never regretted this fact about herself. That is, until now.

Anika watches her husband as he carefully takes another baby blanket down from the display next to the window. This one is decorated with teddy bears, all descending to an unknown destination in pink and blue parachutes. Her husband scratches his beard as he considers the blanket. He tightens his lips into a straight line and slowly runs his hand over the blanket's fuzzy surface.

They've been shopping for quite a while and Anika can't believe he's even taking the time to consider this one. Even at the size it is now, its folded-up size, this blanket is *way* too big. Obscenely big, really. She eyes the door. She wants to leave, walk out into the gently falling snow, and forget the task that is ahead of them both. Tomorrow, they will be going to the hospital, where Anika will be induced. They tell her it will take about twenty-four hours for her baby to be born. Her baby has died, and it will be a quick hello and a long goodbye.

Jake takes two corners of the blanket between his fingers and lets it fall open in front of him. He raises his eyebrows at Anika. She looks at the blanket and imagines the gray and grainy ultrasound image that she saw just yesterday. A little black spot, signifying a heartbeat, was supposed to be flickering in the middle of her baby's chest, but it wasn't.

"I'm sorry," the doctor had said, "I wish I could tell you I see a heartbeat, I really wish I could." After the cold jelly had been wiped off of Anika's stomach and she had pulled her shirt down and gotten herself into a chair, the doctor had described to Anika what to expect when she finally holds the baby in her arms. "The baby will be very small. About five inches long." He handed Anika a lavender-colored book with a picture of two empty hands on the cover. He put his hand on her shoulder and the feel of it sent a jolt

Handknit Doll Blanket

A colorful patchwork doll blanket, knitted in a simple garter stitch, adds warmth to an antique toy horse. (Photograph © Chris Hartlove)

through her body. "This book suggests that you bring a blanket to wrap your baby in," he cleared his throat, "it will be something to bring home with you after you say goodbye."

Later, at home, Anika and Jake had put their hands out and had tried to visualize a baby only five inches long. Then they tried to imagine a blanket for a baby that small. "About the size of a washcloth," Anika had said. This moment had been a fuzzy and slow one. Her hands had felt thick and numb as she held them out to consider the size of her unborn child. She was so far inside herself that she had felt like she was speaking to Jake from the bottom of an empty barrel. But still, Jake had been with her. He knew how tiny their child was going to be.

Now, Anika's husband is looking down at the teddy bear blanket and shaking it a little to get the wrinkles out. "What do you think?" he whispers.

"Hon, it's too big," she whispers back. Anika glances over at the store clerk, who is bent over next to the register, peering over her glasses as she writes. Anika is glad for the large coat she has on; it hides her stomach. She doesn't want to answer any painful questions.

The store is in an old renovated Victorian house, and Anika grabs the fabric of Jake's coat and pulls him over to the bottom of a stairway. A cheerful pink sign with an arrow pointing upward exclaims "More Baby Clothes Up Here!"

"Look, I don't think we're going to find anything. They just don't make blankets that small." Anika pauses for a moment. "I think we should go."

Her husband folds the blanket back up again, adjusting it a little each time as he makes a crease.

"This is important to me. I think we should keep looking," Jake holds the folded blanket against his chest. Anika takes a deep breath. She looks out the window by the door. The branches of pine trees sag to the ground under the

Comfort and Joy

The "Knitting Primer" pattern book, a complete compendium of fifty stitch patterns, encourages knitting aficionados to knit the sampler afghan as a lasting record of their skill.

weight of the wet snow. The air inside the old house feels hot and dry.

"This is important to me too," she says, "but everything is so big, it just doesn't make any sense. What are we going to do?" Jake bites his bottom lip and then runs his hand along the side of his face.

"We'll find something, don't worry. I'm sure there has to be something."

Anika follows Jake back into the main part of the store. The clerk looks up from her bookwork and smiles at Anika. The woman removes her glasses and lets them hang by a beaded chain. Anika does her best to smile back, but then she quickly looks away.

"Can I help you find anything?"

Anika is forced to turn and look at her. They are the only three in the store, so it is very quiet. Anika hears her husband's coat as it rustles and then stops. She is about to tell the clerk that they are just looking, thank you very much, but Jake answers first. She gets this heavy feeling in her chest, and her legs feel weak.

"Are these all the blankets you have?" Jake asks as he points toward the display by the window at the front of the store.

"There are also a few over here," the woman turns and bends over a small table in the corner. "Oh, now look, this one here is especially nice. It was knitted by hand." The woman opens the blanket in front of her and it falls past her knees. They all look at a picture of giraffes and elephants heading into an arc two by two. "Feel how soft it is," she holds the blanket out for Anika to touch. Anika keeps her hands at her side.

The woman withdraws the blanket. "Well anyway, I bought this one for my niece and she just loves it. Carries it with her everywhere!"

"Do you have anything smaller?" Jake asks. The woman considers for a moment with her hand over her mouth.

"No. No, I'm afraid not. Is it some kind of a receiving blanket you're looking for?"

"Well, something like that, but smaller," Jake says.

"No, I'm afraid not," says the woman. "We don't have anything like that here."

Of course they don't. Anika's throat tightens and she feels her face get hot. She focuses her eyes on the trees outside the window. Things like this don't exist in stores. Things like this are custom made, but there isn't time for that. Anika turns and heads for the door, but after a few steps she realizes that Jake isn't following her. He just stands there, his eyes still scanning the shelves. The woman turns back towards the counter and picks up a white piece of paper. She holds it towards Jake and he startles.

"Sorry we don't have what you're looking for. But stop in again. We have a sale coming up. The details are on the flyer," she motions the paper towards Jake again, urging him to take it.

"Yeah. Well, thanks. Thanks a lot." Jake takes the paper and the woman turns to Anika and smiles.

The woman walks to the window and turns the sign over from "Open" to "Closed." The door makes a chiming sound as Anika and Jake walk out onto the front porch. The sky is darkening and the ground is taking on the hue of the moon. The remnants of a circular garden are covered in patches of snow. A large brown sunflower is wearing a crown of white. Jake checks his watch.

"When does the mall close?"

"Jake, I don't want to go to the mall."

"But we need a blanket."

"My God, Jake, don't you get it? A blanket for this baby doesn't exist."

"But then we'll make due. There has to be something we can buy."

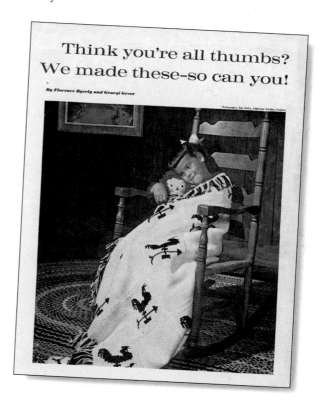

Ideal for Snuggling
A young girl snuggles under a handknit afghan in this 1961 Better Homes and Gardens advertisement.

Woolies from Toyland
Children on the cover of this vintage British pattern book model two of the colorful, nursery-rhyme-themed cardigans that can be made using the patterns inside.

"Like what? Tell me what we can buy, Jake. Tell me."

"I don't know. A cloth. A handkerchief. Something."

Anika shakes her head back and forth and she can't stop shaking it. "No. Absolutely not. No. I don't want to make due. My baby deserves a blanket. Not a handkerchief. Not something you blow your god damn nose in or dust furniture with."

Anika is trembling and she pushes her fingertips into her eyelids to hold back the tears. Jake reaches over and touches the side of her face. Anika steps closer to Jake, leans into him, and puts her head on his shoulder. "I want a real blanket for my real baby."

***

At home, Anika sits on the bed in her pajamas as she watches Jake fill an overnight bag. He puts in his toothbrush, his electric beard trimmer, some jeans, a sweater, some sweat pants. When he's done he sits down next to Anika. She leans into him and puts her head on his shoulder. For the time being, there are no more tears. Just waiting. Jake puts his am around her and rests his head on top of hers.

"Eight o'clock, right?" he asks.

"Uh huh," says Anika. "We should get up around six thirty."

Jake moves away from Anika and reaches over to the nightstand to set the alarm clock. He pushes a button to check the time. It says six thirty. Then he checks it again. They both stare at the wall.

The phone starts to ring. They look at each other and Anika shakes her head no. Anika has been refusing to answer the phone since returning from the doctor's office. She made a couple of phone calls to relatives, but that was it. How could anyone have anything to say to her? She will never have anything in common with anyone ever again. They wait in silence until the ringing stops. Anika gets up and starts to pack her things.

"We should get some sleep," Jake says.

"I'll be done packing in a minute," says Anika. Jake has left one half of the duffle bag empty. Anika puts in some clothes, her toothbrush, a hairbrush, and some make-up. She stays on her knees and stares at the bag. The most important thing is still missing. Anika imagines a small, new blanket, clean and unmarked by anything but her baby's skin. She imagines soft yarn knitted by her own hands. She knows that a lot of people knit things while they wait for their baby to be born. Booties and things like that. She cringes. Not her, she has never been the type. She can't quite get herself to zip up the bag, so she leaves it like it is. When she looks up, Jake is laying on the bed, with his arm draped over his eyes. A small lamp on the nightstand is the only thing lighting the room. Everything looks small and shadowy.

In bed, Anika pictures the day ahead, but her mind will only go so far. A hospital, white sheets, nurses, and doctors. Jake rolls closer and puts his arm over her. He smoothes her hair down and then lays his face close to hers. She feels herself retreating but tries to stay with him. She needs him. She turns her head and kisses his forehead.

"I love you," she says.

"I love you too." There is nothing in the silence but their breathing.

"It doesn't feel real," says Jake.

Anika wonders if it ever will.

"We can get through this, I know we can," says Jake.

Anika rolls over on her side and curls her legs up against Jake. Jake smoothes her hair down again but says nothing more. The waiting is almost over.

***

The morning is impossibly cold and Anika can see her breath as they walk up to the entrance of the hospital. They had been here once before. They had taken a group tour of the maternity floor a month ago when they were trying to decide which hospital to use for the birth. Even so, neither of them can quite remember what floor they need to be on.

"I think that Dr. Pettit told me the ninth floor," says Anika.

"That seems right," says Jake, "the ninth floor. That's where we toured. That's the maternity floor."

Anika stops walking and turns to Jake. "But no, then that can't be right." Anika's breath forms a growing cloud in front of her face. "They wouldn't have me on the maternity floor, would they? Not with all the mothers."

Jake raises his shoulders and rubs his hands together to keep them warm. He looks at her apologetically. "Hon, I'm not sure. We'll see when we get there."

They make their way across the sidewalk to the revolving door. Overnight, the wet snow has frozen. Jake reaches out to Anika's elbow to steady her as she walks across the slippery ice. Anika wonders if he realizes that he doesn't have to do this for her anymore. It doesn't matter so much if she falls.

They walk past the security guard and then the gift shop. They follow the signs to the elevator and push the up button. When they get on the elevator, a man in a blue uniform with a large box on a dolly rushes down the hall and into the elevator with them.

"Which floor?" he says and smiles.

"Ninth," says Jake. The man pushes nine and five. Jake takes the duffle bag off his shoulder and holds it by the straps.

"Have a nice day," the man says over his shoulder, and the door closes. Anika grabs Jake's hand and holds on tight.

When the door opens at the maternity floor, they both step into the hallway and look around. A pregnant woman is making her way slowly down the hall in a hospital gown and light-blue slippers. She stops, puts her hands on her stomach, and breathes her way through a contraction. Somehow, Anika makes her legs carry her past this woman. Finally, they come to a long desk with a lot of nurses in colorful lab coats. Nobody notices them at first. Anika sees that one nurse is looking down at another nurse's feet.

"Did you get new shoes?" the one asks the other, who is writing on a clipboard.

"Yeah, I hit a sale last week," she says and clicks her pen. They both look up and when they see Anika and Jake, they stop what they are doing immediately.

"How can we help you?" says one of the nurses.

"I'm Anika. Anika Johnson." The nurse clicks the mouse at the computer and then stands up fast.

"You're over on the other side," she says, "I'll show you where." She comes around the desk and walks Anika and Jake down a large hallway. The floor shines under the fluorescent lights. Another pregnant woman is holding the small of her back. A husband is whispering softly. Anika

wipes tears from the corners of her eyes. She wants to be in a room. Any room. Fast. They stop at another desk. She hears the nurse say, "This is Anika Johnson."

A hand is on the small of her back. She is being lead to a door. It has a small picture taped under the number, a small watercolor painting of a flower. Suddenly Anika remembers the group tour. A man had asked, "Why does this door have a flower?" The tour guide said, "Because the baby inside is stillborn. It's a sign for the staff." The group fell silent and moved on and Anika wondered how anyone could possibly endure such a thing.

Now, Anika is the woman with the stillborn.

Tears fall fast and Anika has no sense of physical space anymore. She could even be floating. She's not sure. Someone helps her into a chair with a vinyl cushion. She breathes and a hand produces a tissue. Someone is blowing their nose and the sound makes Anika look up. The room steadies itself. It's Jake, wiping his eyes and blowing his nose. A woman in blue scrubs is standing in front of a dresser that is built into the wall. She smiles slightly and cocks her head at Anika. She puts her hand on Jake's shoulder and then walks over to the door and shuts it softly. Anika is relieved to have the bustle of the hospital shut off from them.

"My name is Susan," says the nurse, "And first of all I just want to say how sorry I am."

"Thank you," says Anika as she looks down at her tissue. She doesn't know what else to say. What else is there to say?

"I'll be here through the whole birth," says the nurse. "And I want you to know that I can answer any questions you might have."

Jake sits in a chair next to Anika. He looks up at the nurse.

"When will Dr. Pettit be here?"

"Any minute now. He called to say he's stuck in traffic. But it shouldn't be too much longer."

People are stuck in traffic. People are rushing to work, to the laundromat, to the grocery store. It seems crazy, really. Crazy that everyone isn't just frozen in place with the fragility of life. Anika blows her nose and then clears her throat. All eyes are on her, waiting for her to say something.

"The doctor gave us a book," Anika says and the nurse

Bands of Color

A pair of brightly colored Oleana afghans, designed by Solveig Hisdal, are sure to warm both the body and the spirit of those who nestle under them. (Photograph © Solveig Hisdal)

raises her eyebrows. "And it says that we should have brought some kind of blanket to wrap the baby in. But all the blankets are so big, and, well, we didn't know what to bring."

"We have a packet for you," says the nurse. "There may be something in there like that. I'll be right back." The nurse opens the door to the blended sounds of voices and footsteps. Jake and Anika look out the window. The sky is gray and small flakes are falling again and blowing diagonally

New Lux Knitting Book
The 1952 edition of the New Lux Knitting Book *includes directions for a cozy interwoven blanket for baby.*

past the window. The nurse returns and they both stand up. She hands Anika and Jake a white bag made out of quilted fabric.

Anika sits down on the hospital bed and Jake takes the bag and sits down next to her. Jake puts the bag in his lap and undoes the Velcro at the top. They both peer inside. Jake pulls out a small, yellow blanket and lays it in between them on the bed. Anika reaches over and slowly unfolds it. It's a small square, about the size of a washcloth. There is a tag, cut with a fancy border, attached with a ribbon to the corner of the blanket. Anika reads the words:

> Keepsake Baby Afghan
> Stitched with love by the
> Cambridge Church knitting group

She wipes the blur from her eyes. She fingers the loose stitch and then runs her hand over the surface of the blanket. Jake begins to sob but eventually she can hear him taking deep breaths. She rubs the top of his thigh. The nurse leaves the room and shuts the door, and once again the noises of the hospital are cut off from them both. Anika lays her hand on the blanket and lets her fingertips move around the yarn in small circles. She imagines women knitting. Sipping coffee and knitting blankets for babies that they aren't afraid to visualize, aren't afraid to picture the size of.

Anika picks the blanket up and lets the weight of it lie on both of her palms. Then she spreads the blanket gently on her lap. She stares at it for a long time. She runs her fingertips along a line of stitches and she notices that not even this blanket is without its own imperfection. Not every stitch is exactly the same size, nor is every stitch as round as the next. But the women keep on knitting anyway, finding some sort of solace in their act, some kind of relief in their creation.

Anika looks outside again at the snowflakes swirling back and forth beyond her window. She and Jake are very quiet. Anika runs her fingertips over the stitches as she watches the snow and listens to a clock ticking out sounds like the rhythm of clicking needles.

A Bouquet of Yarns

Bouquet knitting wools, available in a variety of fun colors, are guaranteed not to shrink or stretch with wear.

CHAPTER 4

THE ART OF KNITTING

AS A CHILD, I USED RAINY SUNDAYS TO VISIT MUSEUMS. THE HISTORICAL MUSEUM IN BERGIN HAD ITS OWN SECTION ON FOLK ART; MANY DARK ROOMS WITH ROSE-PAINTED (ROSEMALING) CHESTS, BEDS, AND CUPBOARDS. . . . WHEN I BEGAN TO DESIGN KNITWEAR, IT WAS NATURAL TO RETURN TO THE MUSEUM TO GATHER INSPIRATION. A VISIT TO THE MUSEUM WAREHOUSE IS LIKE ENTERING PARADISE.

–Solveig Hisdal, Poetry in Stitches, 2000

Sweaters, mittens, and scarves are seldom the first thing that comes to mind when one thinks of an art museum. Although knitting has achieved some recognition as an art form in recent years, the craft still has a utilitarian reputation. People began to knit to create practical garments with the sole purpose of keeping warm, not necessarily to make something beautiful. Today, knitting is very much about both—creating something beautiful that may be worn or displayed as art. Knitting is sculptural, sensual, colorful, *and* useful. As knitting has become more popular, the art of such knitting designers and fiber artists as Debbie New, Karen Searle, and Solveig Hisdal has found its way into galleries and museums. Knitting is an art whose time has come.

"Knitting Girl"
In this serene painting, completed by William Adolphe Bourguereau in 1869, a young girl rests against a tree trunk as she knits a sweater sleeve on double-point needles.

Minerva Yarns
A new skein of China-blue Minerva yarn patiently waits for a knitter to rip off the paper label, pull the tail from the center of the ball, and begin to knit.

Knit Gallery: The Search for a Proper Place among the Arts

By Teva Durham

Why is knitting considered less of an art than painting, sculpting, or weaving? In "Knit Gallery: The Search for a Proper Place among the Arts," knitwear designer and writer Teva Durham struggles to understand knitting's lowly reputation among the arts. A more condensed version of this essay appeared in Interweave Knits' Ravelings column in the fall 2003 issue. Teva wrote for Vogue Knitting and interned with Dana Buchman before she started Loop-d-loop, a company dedicated to raising respect for the art of knitting. Loop-d-loop sells Teva's knitting patterns and supplies pattern kits to knitters. Teva continues to contribute knitting-related articles to knitting magazines and books.

My mother who owns a studio school/gallery introduces me at openings as "My daughter, the knitter." I glare at her surreptitiously, as daughters will do. The description sounds so, well, domestic and when I attempt to elaborate on the extent of my career to whoever has given a polite response ("That's cool, I know some girl who knits" or "I used to knit or was that crochet?" or "Didn't I just read it's coming back?") it is awkward because she has played it down so much, making it sound like my hobby. The momentary dismissal seen in the stranger's eyes begins to change to bewilderment, then interest. Yet I feel it is not the response I would get if I were called a "fiber artist" sculpting totems out of wads of felt or if I were presented as a "fashion designer" working in cut and sew fabrics. But I am both a fiber artist and a fashion designer. What is the stigma of handknitting that drags it down a notch? It's not just that you wear the results—making it not pure, not art for art's sake, not cerebral, but utilitarian and mundane—or fashion designers wouldn't be so esteemed. Could it be knitting is tainted by traditionally being third world or woman's work, "handiwork," "craft," and thus neither "art" nor the modern, sleek, media-friendly term "design"? And when I try to explain my audience, that for the most part I create items for enthusiasts to replicate or improvise on, why does it seem to devalue my work more, associating it with paint-by-numbers, rather than being tantamount to a composer

Homage to the Goddess, Creation
One of a series of goddess thrones created by fiber artist Karen Searle, this work of art is made of tablet-woven silk, metallic threads, and beads that have been knitted and crocheted around a chair frame. This creation honors creation myths and legends from many cultures in a folk-art style. (Photograph © Karen Searle)

whose pieces are played? Is it my personal self-esteem problem or is knitting, even with the recent hype and popularity, a mouse among arts?

"Next time, Mom," I plead, "Can you call me a designer, at least?"

"But Dear, you are a knitter. It is best to be modest and be proud of the craft you've pursued."

Once, she did admit that, perhaps, in our family of artists I have been the most successful at my creative endeavor. This did not sit well with me either. I suddenly felt guilty about the years of knowledge in anatomy, composition and draftmanship my parents possess—maybe that adds up to more than being able to decipher any cable and turn it into a chart or invent new stitch patterns. Of course it is not a competition, but an artistic family is by definition a narcissistic family and there is inherent pressure to get attention and to make a mark. My father, a retired art department chairman whose days as a promising young painter in a spattered and torn t-shirt, brandishing his brushes are part of the family lore, now puts knitting magazines on his coffee table and shows them to his guests; he keeps tabs on my submissions and emails his buddies with the latest. It is so embarrassing.

To sort out these feelings, I've been examining how my artistic value system was formed. Being raised by artists afforded me a childhood rich in the senses, filled with ideals my sensitive, silly girl mind tried to grasp. I've been revisiting the days before I went to school and tried to blend in with "ordinary" people. In my family art was like religion and I figured out early on that, just as in a church, art had a hierarchy. We actually didn't attend church, but Our Lady of Lourdes was up the hill at the end of the block and because my mother had gone there as a girl (she had scars on her knees from all the kneeling) it held endless fascination for me. Although I played with neighborhood children, I felt different and excluded—we were special because Dad was an artist. Mom was an artist also—they met in art school—but firstly, and this was how I wanted it, she was a housewife. My father had converted the garage into a studio and its lofty roof reminded me of a steeple. He carried the studio's mysterious scent with him through the house: a pungent blend of oils and turpentine, which I knew to be

poison. He would take his cups of coffee back there where we wouldn't disturb him and do his abstract expressionist work that looked like a big scribble filled with different patterns. My mother, in stolen moments, poured her creative energy into small projects—her quite brilliant attempts at children's books would be hidden away in a drawer when they met with disinterest—and she did pastel portraits at street-fairs and parties often while we restless kids clung to her skirt. My mother sometimes taught children's art classes, whereas my father taught at The College. My

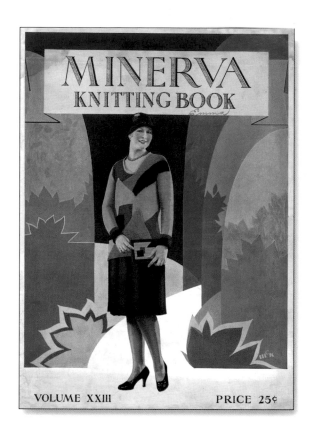

1928 Minerva Knitting Book
The cover of this pattern book, steeped in the Art Nouveau style so popular during the 1920s, is a work of art in itself.

Tribute to Flowers
Worked in a rich palette of yellows and reds, this sweater designed by Solveig Hisdal was inspired by a hand-painted wooden trunk on display at the Vestvågøy Museum in Norway. (Photograph © Solveig Hisdal)

Peacock Coat, 1997
This vivid cape, designed by Debbie New, is knitted in mohair and lined with chiffon. Debbie began by knitting the medallions before linking them to one another with strips of swirl knitting. (Photograph © Sandy Nicholson Photography)

father taught something called Composition, which was something like the sky is up and the grass is down and it seemed if we didn't have it we'd be Chicken Little. I remember when my Dad had a show in a bank building—getting all dressed up, watching him knot his tie, taking in the nervous excitement of the long ride in the station wagon, seeing at close range, thigh level his polyester houndstooth pleated pants and her Marimekko print dress, peering up at the fizzing drink glasses. Many times the grownups talked late into the night when I had to be upstairs in bed. Art seemed such a serious struggle and it got them so excited. They talked of Gaslight Square (I imagined a six-inch square, set ablaze), which had been to St. Louis what Greenwich Village was to New York in the sixties. They mentioned all these funny, multisyllabic names with strange flavors—for instance, Kandinsky sounded like a confection with shimmering sparkles. I may have been too young to understand much, but I got that art was about danger, indulgence, celebration, and suffering and was done in special places by exceptional people.

We often visited the St. Louis Art Museum, and my mother worked there for a time. There was an Oldenberg plug sculpture to the side of the building—I enjoyed this giant-sized household object so much and I wondered if there was some reason it didn't belong inside the museum. The art inside was intimidating—all the somber portraits with haunting eyes, the agony and ecstasy in religious scenes, the classical statues of naked women without arms. The museum was a special but somewhat dreaded place for me—the way footsteps echoed in the hush, the guards standing in the doorways, warning not to touch. Even a small bronze cast of Degas' little dancer was scary as she didn't seem to be a doll at all, but a real girl shrunken down—something like the mummy in the Egyptian room whose toe, of the same brown hue, was peeking through the bandages. When I was four or five, somehow I became convinced the Devil lived beneath the museum, even though I had never heard a sermon and we didn't have a television. Then one day while my mother was working, I was allowed to stay in the lobby to watch an exhibit of weavers. A nice lady sat

behind a giant wooden-framed loom, throwing a foot-long shuttle through an opening in the multicolored strings that she created by stepping on a peddle, then taking a giant comb and beating down the strings to form fabric. My mother spoke to the woman and arranged to order a tapestry loom and an inkle loom for me even though they probably cost more than she made that week.

It is easy for me to see how and why I prefer a life of "craft" rather than "art." As a child I used to scribble in imitation of my father's work and look for appreciation. But it was beading and weaving that really got me jumping out of bed in the morning. Now I am kind of having a second childhood, staying up late to see how a new yarn knits up. I've always had a facility and need for that state of concentration, that creative trance that is especially available to children. Robert Henri, an American painter, wrote in *The Art Spirit* (1923), a book once recommended to me by an acting teacher, "The object which is at the back of every work of art, is the attainment of a state of being, a state of functioning, a more than ordinary moment of existence." Knitting transports me in this way; it is consistently a positive force in my life. For many years I pursued acting and writing, because they seemed more worthy arts; I struggled with the insatiable yearning for validation, riding the highs and lows I associated with being an "artist," even though my teachers stressed, and I understood, practicing a craft and enjoying the process. At some point my knitting "hobby" took over my life, and I realized it was a healthier, happier pursuit for me.

Matisse, after completing *La Joie de Vivre* in 1908, called for "an art of balance, of purity and serenity devoid of troubling or depressing subject matter . . . like an appeasing influence, like a mental soother, something like a good armchair in which to rest from physical fatigue." Knitting embodies this for me. The more I master it, the more I see its possibilities and believe it deserves the respect and serious consideration of any art. Knitting doesn't (usually) attempt to convey the tragedy of the human condition, rather, just as importantly, it celebrates being human, exploring the capabilities of our minds and hands. A piece's

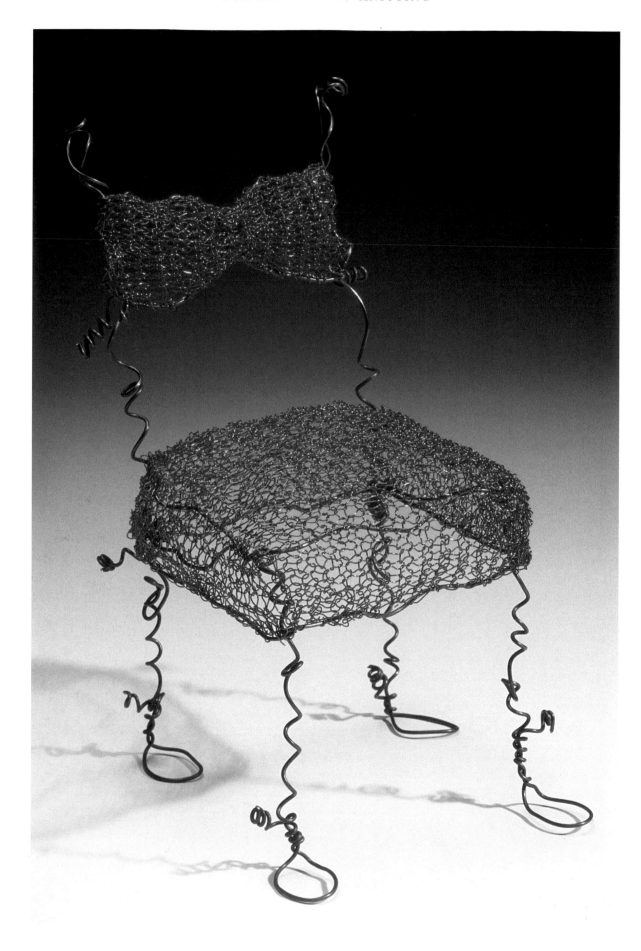

expression is nonverbal, but tells a story much as a canvas can, utilizing form, surface texture, color, composition, etc. Furthermore, the energy of the body is used to create a covering for the body. When we wear a handknit piece it is a dance of energy, it's conceptual art and performance art rolled into one. Why should self-doubt make me cringe at art openings? Obviously, there is a need for a "knitter's lib" movement. Our community is tenuous, existing on the pages of magazines, on the internet, in yarn shops, guild meetings, trade shows, and chance encounters with needles out in public. I feel we aren't making the most of our opportunities and special places. Wouldn't it be fabulous to speak of Norah Gaughan with the same fervor given Gauguin, to study the significance of Kaffe Fassett as some do Faulkner, to discuss late into the night how a knitting pattern can be interpreted like sheet music? Well, maybe there is a danger of changing knitting's tranquil nature by imposing on it the pretense and hero-worship of the art world.

I have a particular affinity for the English and American eccentrics at the turn of the (last) century and the societies, collectives, and communities that cropped up seeking to create an environment where art and craft are integral, where everything shows the artistic detail achieved by hand and is integrated with the nature of its material. This Arts and Crafts Movement was a reaction to the Industrial Revolution which cluttered the daily life of Victorians with shoddily-made, mass-produced items, offending the aesthetic senses of elitist writers like Ruskin, threatening extinction for artisans, as well as causing concern about conditions in factories. It was also, like Modern Art, influenced by exposure to Eastern and "primitive" philosophy and artifacts. Many designers and firms (Tiffany, Stickley, Roycroft) and architects (Frank Lloyd Wright) enjoyed success; the Swedish Bohus knitting workshop has been documented in *Poems of Color* (Wendy Keele, 1995), and there were probably numerous lesser-known knitting collectives. The Bauhaus in Germany was a great design school that produced so many innovative items and allowed fine artists (such as Klimpt) to earn a living with fashion and decorative design. The extraordinary textile designer William Morris in *The Lesser Arts of Life* (1882) stated "not only is it possible to make the matters needful to our daily life works of art . . . there is something wrong in the civilization that does not do this." Oscar Wilde lectured Americans on the virtues of good design: "the artist is not concerned primarily with any theory of life but with life itself, with the joy and loveliness that should come daily on eye and ear." Wilde, directing craftsmen to have at hand images of Greek, Italian and Japanese pieces of timeless beauty, stated "Work in this spirit and you will be sure to be right. Do not copy it, but work with the same love, the same reverence, the same freedom of the imagination." (*Art and the Handicraftsman*, 1908) For the proponents of the Arts and Crafts Movement it was enough for a work of art to be "a well-made thing" where "design interpenetrates the workmanship," showing it was "made by a human being for a human being" (*Art and Workmanship*, W. R. Lethaby, 1915). What could be more applicable to this than knitting?

The next time my mother introduces me to some artist, in front of some savagely glued together, paint-spattered collages of body parts, as "My daughter, the knitter," I will look the other person straight in the eye and proudly say, "Yes, that's me."

Spirit Throne

Created from a bent aluminum frame and knitted copper wire, artist Karen Searle's "Spirit Throne" honors the female spirit.
(Photograph © Karen Searle)

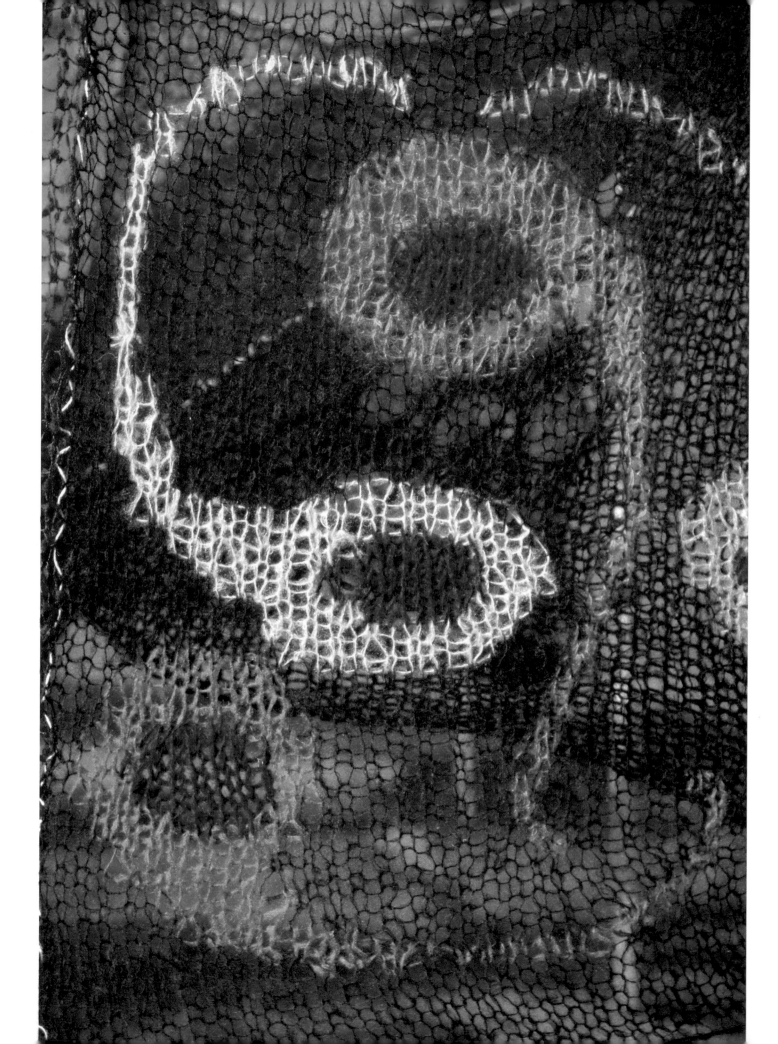

An Ode to the Knit Stitch

By Pam Allen

It's amazing that knitting, as simple as the concept is, can produce such striking results. Each stitch links beautifully with the stitches on either side, yet each stitch has its own, slightly unique character. In "An Ode to the Knit Stitch," Interweave Knits editor and author of Knitting for Dummies Pam Allen urges knitters to look more carefully and with reverence at the art of the knit stitch. She too hopes that knitting will someday receive the recognition it deserves.

Occasionally when I run into someone I've met a while back, they'll say to me, "I remember you; you're the one who weaves." And I assure them that they're half right. I work with yarn. But I'm not a weaver, I knit. In response to this clarification, I often detect a slight slump in the other person, a minor wrinkle in the forehead as they grapple with the idea of knitting as a serious concern. And I feel like my glow has dimmed a bit, as if "knitter" were poor cousin to "weaver." At that moment, I'm grateful that I needn't identify myself as someone who crochets. It seems that in the hierarchy of fiber crafts, weaving, knitting, and crochet might be ranked in the order of Mercedes, Volkswagen, and scooter.

I wonder where we get our ideas about what's important or serious in the world of fiber craft. Does weaving carry more weight because it requires a relatively large and imposing piece of equipment? Does the convenience of knitting, the simple equipment required—a pair of needles, a ball of yarn—limit its status to a craft for simpletons? (If so, the equipment criteria might explain why crochet is even further down the scale—it requires a single hook.) Or is knitting considered homey and unexciting because the universal symbol of the knitted garment is a pair of socks?

For me, the very simplicity of knitting, its immediacy and portability, are part of its appeal. Knitting is the craft of the nomad. Never mind that I have lived in the same house for sixteen years, that I could scarcely begin to carry my collection of needles and yarn from my workroom to the front door. When I leave the house, I carry with me whatever I'm currently working on, usually in a recycled grocery bag. Wherever I am—at a basketball game, waiting for the dentist, in the airport—when my hands pick up and position my needles, when I unwind a little yarn from the ball, when I twine the strand in an unconscious movement around the fingers of my right hand, I put my world in order. I appreciate the know-how in my hands, the rote movement, the kinesthetic connection of yarn, needles, and fingers. As I knit, the unkempt rumple of my inner life, the thoughts and concerns which like to converge willy-nilly to clamor for attention, straighten themselves out in an orderly fashion. I can consider them one at a time, if I want to consider them at all.

The fact of the matter is, simple as the requirements are for a knitted project, there's nothing limited about the creative possibilities of the knitted stitch. For eons, men and women and children have knit garments to wear for

Labyrinth of Rebirth, 2001
One of thirty-three panels designed by Debbie New to depict the various stages of fetal development, this panel represents sperm cells. The panels are knit from mohair and exhibited together in the form of a maze. (Photograph © Sandy Nicholson Photography)

practical warmth and to adorn themselves. A look through any dictionary of knitting patterns will show hundreds of variations on ways to pull a loop through another loop to form a textured material. Any color pattern that can be drawn on a piece of graph paper can be transformed into a knitted fabric. One can knit on a miniature scale with thread using wire for needles, and one can knit with rope on pieces of rubber hose. A woven garment requires cutting and sewing, darting and coaxing to take the form of a three-dimensional body. Knitted fabric can be shaped to any outline and constructed with complex dimensional curves and angles built in as it's worked. One can knit a sweater from top to bottom, bottom to top, side to side, and on the diagonal. One can knit in circles, flat, or tube-like. Ingenious knitters have found ways to knit tree houses, tea cups, and masks. Artists have used knitting as an expressive medium to comment and explore the profundity of life and death. Knitting is ancient.

Perhaps I'm so enamored of knitting—the feel and movements of knitting and its structure—because both lend themselves so well to metaphor. Even Shakespeare knew the power of knitting to soothe when he compared it to a good night's sleep that mends "the raveled sleeve of care." And the interlocking looped structure of knitted fabric suggests a model for living in harmony with our neighbors. It's forgiving. Each stitch has its own identity (how often do we notice the one that's slightly out of whack?). Yet each depends upon its neighbors for its integrity. When knitted fabric is stretched, each stitch will give up a part of its share of the common strand of yarn, shrinking slightly with gracious ease to allow the overall fabric to grow as needed. When released, it gracefully returns to its former size.

Do I claim too much for knitting? Perhaps. But I sometimes wonder that people don't look more carefully—and with reverence—at the knitted stitch. When I'm helping someone learn to knit, I can't help telling them to pause once in a while to notice their stitches. Not just the ones on the needles, the ones they're so focused on. I ask them to look at the stitches they've already made and forgotten, the ones that have long since

blended into the whole. The piece of knitted fabric that grows under their needles is not mush, it's a well-engineered construction made up of discreet and identifiable interlocking loops. One needn't look through a microscope to delineate the undulating curves of the single strand of yarn as it loops to form each stitch, appearing as a "v" on one side of the fabric, as a rounded pip on the other. With care, one can follow the flow of the strand of yarn in its rhythmic over, around, down, and over pattern.

Several years ago I visited artist/knitter Katharine Cobey. As I crossed the yard to her studio, I glanced at a simple, curving wire sculpture suspended from a branch of a tree. It wasn't until later, when I was on my way home, that I realized what I had looked at. It wasn't an abstract bending of wire dangling gracefully in space that I had passed under on my way back and forth. Instead, I had walked by a sculptural representation of two knit stitches, two interlocking loops arranged one on top of the other— and I had missed it. There, cast in bronze (so to speak) was the simple element, the basis of so many design possibilities, the repository of so much history, the knitted stitch.

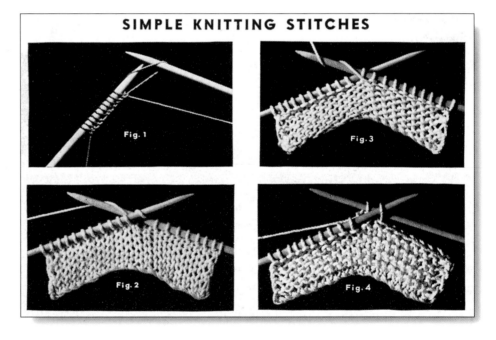

Simple Knitting Stitches

Diagrams, published in a Chadwick's Red Heart Wools pattern book from 1941, illustrate how to cast on, purl, knit, and bind off.

Elven Cloak, 2001
Designed by Debbie New for her book Unexpected Knitting, *the Elven Cloak was knit from metallic thread and sewing cotton, using the scribble lace knitting technique. The result is a delicate, lightweight shawl that is surprisingly warm. (Photograph © Sandy Nicholson Photography)*

Everybody Knit
A pattern book from Australia encourages everyone to be smart and knit with Patons Wools.

Prime of Life
Knitted with linen yarn, this sculpture stands eight inches tall. In creating "Prime of Life," artist Karen Searle wanted to illustrate the beauty of the aging female body. (Photograph © Karen Searle)

Dreaming of Dragons

By Susan Gordon Lydon

Creating a work of art is all about pushing the boundaries and stepping outside one's comfort zone. For longtime knitter and writer Susan Gordon Lydon, this meant reaching beyond Fair Isle knitting, a color work technique with which she felt at home, and into the complicated world of intarsia knitting. In this excerpt from her book The Knitting Sutra: Craft as a Spiritual Practice, *Lydon conquers an intricate and extremely difficult dragon sweater designed by Annabel Fox. She emerges from the project exhausted, but with a new skill—complete comfort with two-handed color technique—a gift in itself.*

I promised myself that when I finished my book I would embark on a sweater project so complex and intricate that it could absorb my total attention. I'd had my eye on something in the Annabel Fox book for quite a while: a swirling pattern of entwined dragons in blues, reds, and ivories on a dark blue ground. The design had been inspired by a Ming vase. Making it involved a kind of color work I had never done before, which looked about as difficult as it's possible for knitting to get. I was somewhat daunted by the prospect of trying it, but the thought of learning something new intrigued me, and I liked the bare bones of the sweater, its lines.

The technique of knitting a picture into fabric is called intarsia. Fair Isle knitting also creates pictures, but its defining quality is that only two colors are used in any given row. With intarsia knitting, each row may contain as many colors as the pattern requires, sometimes quite a large number. I had knitted Fair Isle yokes before but had never attempted anything so complicated as these dragons. When I tried to prepare for it by knitting a multicolored sample swatch, I spent an entire Saturday tangled in yarn, getting nowhere at all. By the end of that day I was so bound up in frustration that with any sense I would have quit right there, but of course I didn't.

Instead I went to the Knitting Basket for help. Sheila, one of the women who works there, who comes from England ("with Irish tendencies," as she says) and has been knitting since childhood, showed me a method for doing color work. Normally I knit Continental style, which means you pick the yarn off the index finger of your left hand, which acts as a shuttle, by moving the needle with your right hand. In American-style knitting, you manually place the yarn around the needle by "throwing" it with your right hand. Sheila told me that in order to do color work I would

Lace Coracle, 1999
Knitted from merino wool and crochet cotton and covered in a fiberglass resin for Meg Swansen's book A Gathering of Lace, *this boat actually floats. Debbie New designed the coracle based on the small round boats used during prehistoric times. (Photograph © Sandy Nicholson Photography)*

have to knit both ways simultaneously, alternating Continental style with my left hand and American style with my right. If this sounds impossibly confusing, imagine how difficult it is to do. The degree of manual dexterity it required boggled my mind; I was in despair of ever being able to learn it. Even after a lifetime of knitting, when I tried to combine the two styles, my fingers felt as stiff and awkward as a beginner's, and I lapsed into utter incompetence.

Still, I am nothing if not tenacious once an obsession has taken root in my mind, and I had fallen in love with a Chinese lacquer red chenille that featured prominently in the pattern. So I went home and practiced. I managed to master at least part of the technique (the other part, for carrying extra yarn neatly behind the work, I still haven't learned to do). Then I decided to start my sweater with a sleeve, which had only a single dragon and looked far easier than the body.

The pattern had been drawn out on graph paper with a series of different typographical symbols (open squares,

Knitter's Dream
Golden rays of sunlight warm the multicolored skeins that stack the shelves of a local yarn shop. (Photograph © Chris Hartlove)

closed squares, circles, and so on) to denote the various colors. I had to enlarge the pattern and fill in the squares with colored pencils before I could even begin to understand what I was supposed to do. Then I had to keep track of what row I was on by having the graph paper spread out before me at all times, weighted down on the sides, with a ruler resting just below the row I was currently working.

One of my favorite things about knitting is the establishing of a rhythm that carries through the work. Rhythm is paramount in producing the psychic serenity that usually accompanies knitting. Just as a shaman will ride a drumbeat out of his body and into the spirit world, a knitter will trail the soothing rhythm of the clicking needles into the deep quiet recesses of her mind.

With the dragon sweater, it was impossible to establish a rhythm, and the work proceeded with such agonizing slowness that I thought I would lose my mind. I could have knit a whole other sweater, with twining cables and twenty different stitch panels, in the time it took me to complete one sleeve. Any given row required between twelve and twenty colors. No sooner had I gone a few stitches with one or two than I had to put them down and pick up new colors, consulting each square of the graphed-out pattern at every turn. Mind you, in knitting one cannot just pick up a color and put it in as would be done in a painting. Each new yarn has to be anchored into the fabric, and the other colors must be carried along the back, loosely enough that they allow the fabric to stretch yet not so loosely that they gap. Attach, knit, strand, twist, carry, stretch the stitches, weave in the thread. And to make matters worse, the balls of colored yarn constantly became entangled and would have to be unwound.

The work was so difficult that I had to talk out loud to myself in order to keep track of the procedure. "Light blue here; strand the red across the back; anchor the red; okay now, pick up the dark blue for two stitches." I felt like a crazy person. I was concentrating so hard to be able to do it that when I put the work down, I could almost feel my mind spring back outward, as though it had been compressed by a giant rubber band. In Arica, Oscar Ichazo had taught us a series of exercises called Kinerhythms, somewhat akin to rubbing your stomach in a counterclockwise motion while patting the top of your head, only more complex and requiring more intense focus. He said that these exercises, when

Duet for Thread and Theremin, 1996
Debbie New knit mixed fibers within a framework of tulle and plastic tubing to create this colorful tribute to the Theremin, an instrument developed in 1920 in Russia by a man of the same name. The Theremin at the base of this piece was built by New, and it emits unique sounds whenever someone touches the knitted fibers. (Photograph © Brian Céré of Dumont Group Photography, Kitchener, Ont.)

mastered, would "make the brain sing." That's how I felt about the dragon sweater. Only it wasn't making my brain sing; it was making it groan in anguish.

After a weekend of struggling with the sleeve, I went back to the Knitting Basket on Monday. This time Linda showed me how to cut lengths of yarn for each color so that the strings trailed off the bottom of the row and were far easier to untangle than balls of yarn or bobbins. Two indispensable tips had now been provided to me by the knitting ladies to ease this difficult project, yet each time I worked on it my head still felt like it was going to explode.

***

In Chinese culture the dragon is a powerful totem. It symbolizes heaven, the ethereal realms of the spirit. The dragon chases the pearl of wisdom in an eternal quest for enlightenment. In ancient times only royal figures were permitted to wear the dragon on their clothing, as it was thought to bestow upon the wearer the power of heaven. It's interesting that the Chinese chose a mythological creature to symbolize the spiritual realms, as both are unseen and therefore must be imagined. A willingness to believe in what cannot be seen is a cornerstone of the spiritual life. We may take on faith or grasp by intuition the existence of

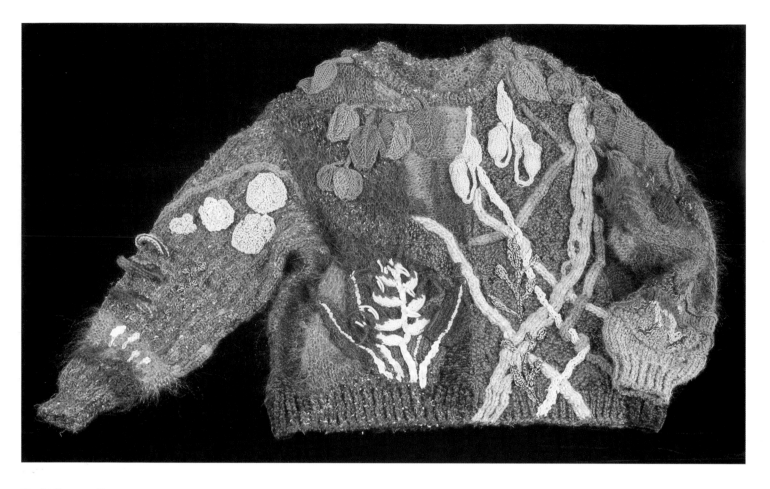

Rainforest Sweater, 1994

Ferns, fungi, vines, a poison dart frog, and an eyelash viper decorate this sculptural Debbie New sweater that pays tribute to the rainforest. (Photograph © Brian Céré of Dumont Group Photography, Kitchener, Ont.)

that which we cannot see; either way a belief in it stands firmly at odds with the empirical scientific view of the Western mind-set.

In Western mythology dragons were more often seen as symbols of fear or superstition. Ancient maps faded out at the edges of the known world with the legend "Here there be dragons." In Christianity St. George slew the dragon and vanquished the forces of ignorance. So one might say that Europeans viewed the imaginative and mythological world as inferior knowledge from the past that had been supplanted by superior wisdom culled from scientific exploration and experimentation. Eastern philosophy, on the other hand, saw in this imaginative world the possibility for expanding the limited horizons of the physical plane into infinite areas of transcendental knowledge. Of course, of the two, I vastly preferred the Eastern view. I wanted the pearl without price, the one the dragon chased through the heavens.

The quest for enlightenment leads into the interior; it is a matter of charting the unknown reaches of the inner world instead of believing that the outer world—what you can see and touch with your senses—is all there is. As one Native American teacher, Blackwolf Jones, puts it, the quest for enlightenment is "the path that leads to the center of your being." The path is internal and filled with the inexplicable and the unexpected. Buddhists know that one can never understand the full dimensions of reality with just the rational mind. That is the purpose of the Zen koan, an unanswerable question such as "What is the sound of one hand clapping?" With the koan the teacher shocks the student's mind into an awareness of its own absurdity. Only when the student is able to admit the possibility that she may not know what she thought she did does real learning become possible.

***

As I worked on this almost impossibly difficult sweater in a fever of intense concentration, I seemed to become inhabited by dragons. I began to see them everywhere, and they even surfaced in my dreams. Suddenly I noticed dragons twining around elaborately tattooed arms. I recalled dragon references in drug lingo: addicts who smoked Persian heroin by melting it on tinfoil and drawing off the smoke with a tube called it "chasing the dragon"; others called opium "dragon seed." I remembered my daughter in high school playing "Dungeons and Dragons," and I recalled the long bedtime story she and an ex-boyfriend of mine had concocted together, "The Story of Marbel and Bellina," which featured a friendly dragon not unlike the famous Puff. Chinese vases in shop windows I passed suddenly jumped into my field of vision, and I paused to admire carvings in ivory and jade. The front panel of my sweater was anchored by a dragon that moved horizontally by curling its body up and down in ridges like a black mamba snake. At night while I slept, this dragon came alive and lumbered across the landscape of my dreams.

Making the sweater was unlike any knitting I had experienced before. It was more like weaving a picture or accumulating the tiny stitches of petit point into a painted impressionist effect. I wrestled with colossal effort every time I sat down to work. When I brought the sweater to Florida to work on at my parents' house, my mother was so flabbergasted she was speechless. She didn't have to speak, however, because I knew what she was thinking, and the same thing was on my mind. Why was I doing this? What was the point? The work was excruciating; a full day's knitting would sometimes produce only one inch of sweater. Yet the dragons steadily grew. One progressed in its funny up-and-down motion; another whipped across the sky. I made myself keep working no matter how I felt: my back hurt, my neck hurt, my eyes hurt, my brain hurt. Unless one had done it oneself, I found myself thinking, no one could possibly imagine what heroics could go into a piece of knitting.

But I knew why I was doing it and why I couldn't give up. I had determined to become a master knitter, which meant I would have to acquire competence in many types of knitting. More important than the technical skills, however, I would have to achieve self-mastery, mastery over myself. In the martial arts, one studies fighting techniques to defeat the enemy within, by building character and developing integrity, discipline, judgment, balance, restraint,

Little Black and White Number, 1996
This dazzling cocktail dress began as a few free swirls before Debbie New knitted them together to shape the garment. Created for her book Unexpected Knitting, the dress is made with acrylic yarn. (Photograph © Sandy Nicholson Photography)

and other valued inner attributes. Tai chi, for example, also known as Supreme Ultimate Boxing, is a spiritual as well as a physical discipline, rooted in principles as much as in movement. Though I hadn't known it when I started the sweater, I had embarked on a sort of internal training. And though the work was sometimes torturous, I had to see it through to the end.

I know for a fact that the quality of my work on the dragon sweater is crude and amateurish. Different knitters favor different types of knitting, and someone practiced in color work and intarsia would have done a far better job.

But although I love the sweater, despite or perhaps because of the difficulty of its execution, the finished product seems almost beside the point. The purpose of making the sweater seemed rather in being willing to learn something new, no matter how awkward it felt, and to follow wherever it took me. The point was to open my mind to the presence of dragons in symbology, in design, in language, in myths, in my dreams. The importance of doing it was in achieving self-mastery, forging the discipline to keep on working even when it was hard. And the funny thing about that last part is that self-mastery is precisely the quality that will eventually lead you to the heavenly realms, the ones where dragons play.

***

Don't let me overdo it on the heroism here, though, because once I had sweated and groaned through the front of the sweater and both the sleeves, there was simply no power on heaven or earth strong enough to make me go through that again. Linda and I worked out a compromise where I would knit only one dragon on the back of the sweater, the undulating bottom fellow, and do the rest in solid blue. What a relief! The sweater might still be sitting unfinished in my knitting bag even now if we hadn't decided on that shortcut. One thing I learned while making that sweater is that intricate intarsia color work, though I love its finished results, is simply not for me. Two beautiful Annabel Fox projects currently languish unfinished in my house, and God knows when I'll have the strength to try them again.

The actual knitting benefit I received from the dragon sweater turned out to be entirely unexpected, not at all what I had set out to accomplish. I didn't even realize what it was until after several years had passed. What I'd actually learned was fluency with the two-handed color technique of switching between Continental- and American-style knitting. When it came time to apply it to something I truly loved, traditional Fair Isle knitting, the technique no longer felt awkward and strange. I had done so much of it that by now it came naturally to me; I could switch back and forth at will between the two styles because my hands remembered what they had done. I'd received a sort of initiation by ordeal and had managed to walk off with the prize, the pearl of wisdom, if you will. I was now a practiced two-handed knitter, firmly imbued with the ambidextrous magic, a gift from Sheila, my own hard work, and the dragons who had lumbered through my dreams.

Labyrinth of Rebirth, 2001

Thirty-three colorful mohair panels flap in the breeze like clothes on a line. In its entirety, Debbie New's "Labyrinth of Rebirth," featured in her book Unexpected Knitting, traces the mystery of fetal development, from conception to birth. (Photograph © Sandy Nicholson Photography)

Doreen

2 Needle Socks

BY NELL ARMSTRONG

VOL. 93 20¢

Easy to Knit ON 2 NEEDLES ONLY!

Knitting Socks for the Revolution

By Sigrid Arnott

Who knits socks when you can buy three pairs for five dollars at Target? Sigrid Arnott answers that question logically and eloquently in "Knitting Socks for the Revolution." Her response is rooted in the obvious: knitter's knit for the pure enjoyment of it, for the love of the art. Sigrid is a recovering archaeologist who knits, sews, and writes from her dining room table. She lives in Minneapolis with her fiber-enlightened husband and two young sons.

Between the darkness and the campfire smoke, the knitter's eyes tear up as she tries to see the gray stitches to turn the heel, yet she works on, knitting homespun yarn into scratchy socks for the revolution. Her dearest, the revolutionary leader, sits alongside, waterproofing his army boots, his toes and heels pathetically showing through holes in his cotton socks. Her gaze shifts from her bicycle-spoke needles to his bearded face, aglow with The Cause. Freedom fighters need warm, wool-clad feet to save the oppressed.

Well, forget that fantasy. I am knitting for my own revolution.

I sit in a comfortable chair at home, bathed in lamplight. I'm knitting soft merino wool in hand-painted reds and greens. I don't appear to be defying authority, unless you consider that I wrap the yarn the "wrong" direction around my needles. My manifesto is a well-worn copy of Elizabeth Zimmerman's *Knitting Without Tears*. My activist friends view my apparent apathy with derision. Yet, in my own way, I am leading my own insurrection.

I was standing at the cutting counter of my local fabric store when I realized I am a revolutionist. While chatting with the other crafters who formed an orderly assembly as they waited to have their bolts cut, I happened to mention that I mend socks. How our conversation got that far, I don't remember, but even this motley group of sewers, quilters, and fabric junkies seemed shocked. Finally, the no-nonsense cutter pronounced her verdict: "I would *never* mend socks. Why bother when I can buy three pairs of new socks for five dollars at Target?"

"Well, *I* only mend the ones that *I* knit," I said in humble defense.

The ramifications of my new statement were even more horrifying. Who knows what thoughts filled the awkward silence that followed, but I imagined even these fabric folk were thinking what a fool I must be to waste large amounts of time knitting something that is so cheap, so readily available, and generally invisible. Amidst the maelstrom of the silence, I too was struck with a wave of self-doubt. Why do I buy expensive fiber and then knit it into inconspicuous

Two Needle Socks
On the cover of a 1946 pattern book by Nell Armstrong, a young woman adjusts her prize pair of "skating queen" socks after a day at the rink. Skating queen, pattern number 310, is but one of the toe-warming offerings among many in this easy-to-knit collection.

hosiery? Even I have to admit that although I dearly loved my Koigu socks and always made sure to wear them—like a protective talisman for the feet—on days with potential trouble spots, they did wear out long before my SmartWool™ pair.

And then it occurred to me: Ignoring these very reasons *not* to knit was in itself revolutionary.

My dictionary defines "revolutionary" in several ways. A revolution is the creation of radical change through "the forcible overthrow of an established political system by the people governed." A revolution also refers to a cycle, the process of going around and back to a starting point. Now I know most knitters—especially those who prefer circular knitting—would admit to making a lot of revolutions or "rounds," but they would certainly deny there is anything remotely radical about sitting down with their knitting. They obviously aren't toting machine guns through jungles, toppling governments, or smashing the windows of Gap stores.

Footloose and Fancy Free
Variance on a color scheme make for a pair of socks guaranteed to put spring in your step. A pattern for these socks can be found in Melanie Falick's book Kids Knitting. (Photograph © Chris Hartlove)

When you ask sock knitters why they do it, they offer all sorts of rationale. Some say they like portable projects. Others enjoy the technical aspects of this tricky, time-consuming needlework. Still others say socks take less time to craft than sweaters.

But when we labor for hours to create something simple in its beauty just to put on our feet, we have to ignore core beliefs of our consumer culture. Capitalism depends on us to remember that time is money, that assembly lines separating the producer from the end user maximize efficiency, and that the consumer may purchase what is the cheapest—or the most conspicuously expensive—regardless of true value.

Instead of overthrowing the system, knitting socks renders it irrelevant.

To begin with, my purchase of yarn circumvents the discount-store empires. Instead of a Wal-Mart cashier dragging my skeins over a scanner and dumping it into a plastic sack with all the care of someone sorting garbage, I buy my wool at a small, privately owned store. As the shop owner writes up my receipt, we chat about our craft.

Then I knit the socks. I'm not super-skilled, I like fine-gauge yarns and thin needles, and I have two children to "divert" me, so this can take time—a long time. I don't keep track, but if I spend twenty-five hours knitting a sock and multiply that by minimum wage of $5.15, that sock should cost $128.75.

Considering the years of "training" in the highly technical "field" of knitting, I should earn at least the $17.62 per hour that the federal government sets as the wage for, say, a Cable Splicer (whatever *that* is, although by the name alone it seems analogous to knitting). At that rate, my sock's value skyrockets to $440.50. And that's just for one foot.

On the other hand, if a good pair of store-bought SmartWool™ socks costs $15.00, I subtract the $8.00 I paid for yarn, and divide by fifty hours, my time is worth only 14 cents an hour—about 37 times less than minimum wage.

Either way I figure it, sock knitting is economically ridiculous—I am "wasting" billable hours in increments of work weeks. This is the part of sock making that most confounds nonknitters and sets it counter to the cycles of commerce.

By virtue of being "wasted," my time truly becomes my own. When I am really busy and can't knit, I miss the sensation of working on a project that asks only that I sit and ignore time as much as I miss my yarn and needles. Perhaps not surprisingly, it was during a period of my life when I worked for an engineering corporation that required me to account for my time in six-minute increments that I became obsessive about knitting. Hours spent knitting are hours spent luxuriously ignoring the command of the clock.

At the same time that I was forced to give weekly progress percentage completion reports, I had to learn to stop constantly trying to figure what rate of progress I was making on my knitting projects. Unlike sewing, which is subtractive in that one takes material and cuts it down to size before rapid reassembly, knitting is additive. One stitch added to another in hundreds of revolutions creates the fabric of the sock in an organic, foot-shaped tube. I have learned to see progress this way, stitch by stitch, round by round, until something really exciting happens—it's time to turn the heel! By experiencing time stitch by stitch without calculating what it is paying or costing me, time becomes mine alone.

And so, here I sit, happily knitting socks for the revolution. As I cast on, I am nullifying capitalistic concepts of monetary value and wage labor. Knitting and purling my way through the ribbing, I am breaking the shackles of global consumerism and international economics. Turning the heel, time and money are wasted in glorious profligacy and inefficiency is maximized, even celebrated. As I work my way down the foot, shopping as an opiate of the masses is replaced with the excitement of knitting "just a few more rows." Binding off at the toes, my own small revolution is complete.

There I have my sock. I, the producer, am the proud end user. Even when making socks for my significant other, children, or a friend, they can only be given, never sold for their true worth. Something so priceless yet with so little monetary value and with so much of ourselves caught within the stitches can only be a gift.

Maybe Karl Marx was right when he wrote that man may not make history as he wishes, but we can make socks however we like. I suspect that the sock-knitting revolution has been going on for some time, propelled by women who have taken the extra time to make something lovely—instead of something to expediently sell. The needlework might be part of a museum collection, displayed on an ancient altar cloth, or cherished as a family heirloom. Maybe, I'm just hoping, they are the socks on your own two feet.

Smart Accessories

Who could do anything but root for these smart sock designs? From cables to argyle to socks with tassels, you'll find every sock you'll ever want to knit in "Campus Classics for Knitters," a pattern book published in 1940.

Mad about Plaid
Knit him a gift he's guaranteed to like, this advertisement on the back of a 1948 Bear Brand pattern book suggests, knit him a handsome pair of colorful, stylish plaid socks!

Put One Foot in Front of the Other…
La Plata socks, shown here in a variety of color palettes, were designed by Salt Lake City knitter and designer Nancy Bush. The pattern is based on the design of an Anasazi jug, called an olla, that was found in New Mexico's La Plata Valley. (Photograph © Chris Hartlove)

Knitting is a Pleasure with Daphne
In the comfort of her favorite chair, a knitter savors the pleasure of knitting with Daphne-brand crochet wool, one of the most dependable knitting wools offered by Lincoln Mills yarn company.

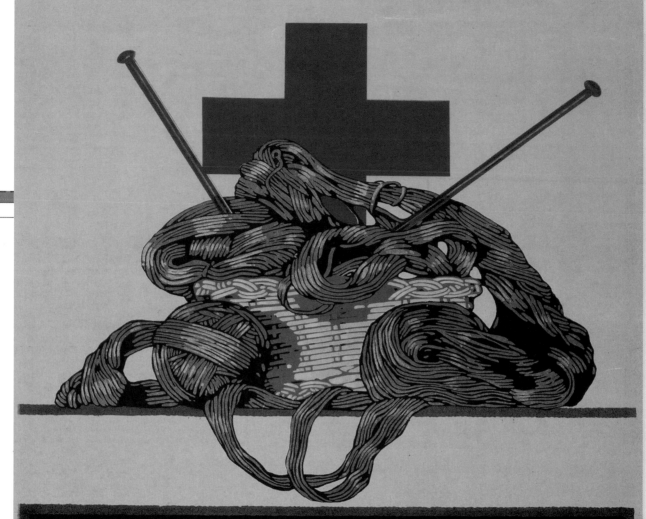

CHAPTER 5

OUR KNITTING HERITAGE

KNITTING FOR ME IS MORE THAN A HOBBY OR LIVELIHOOD. IT IS A MEANS OF BINDING MY LIFE TOGETHER WITH THE LIVES OF ALL KNITTERS, MEN AND WOMEN, WHO HAVE KNIT BEFORE ME—FROM THOSE INDIVIDUALS WHO DISCOVERED HOW TO MAKE INTERLOCKING LOOPS WITH FINGERS AND HOOKED ENDS OF STICKS, TO THOSE COUNTRY FOLK WHO MADE THEIR LIVELIHOOD SELLING HAND-KNIT STOCKINGS FAR FROM THEIR OWN LAND.

—Nancy Bush, from Knitting: History, Fashion, and Great Knitting Yarns, 2000

Knitting for Her True Love
Valentines and postcards depicting young girls knitting for their beloved soldiers on the front lines were popular during World Wars I and II.

Knit Your Bit
During the World Wars I and II, the American Red Cross launched a massive campaign to urge everyone to knit for the boys overseas, hanging posters like these all around the country.

From the time the very first knitter picked up two needles and a ball of yarn and began to knit, the craft has been passed down from generation to generation. In times of war or economic hardship, Red Cross volunteers taught many men, women, and children how to knit, so that they might create sweaters, caps, mittens, and gloves for soldiers fighting overseas. This spirit of giving is still very much a part of the knitting community today. With the surge in knitting's popularity over the past few years, knitters have worked together to stitch afghans and other items to donate to organizations and people in need all over the world. And although it is less common than it once was for mothers to teach their daughters to knit, the skill is being passed down by other means. Those new to knitting are learning in community education classes, at workshops offered at yarn shops, through lessons from friends, or, if they're lucky, through Meg Swansen's annual Knitting Camp. The efforts of those who teach knitting, whether in an official or casual setting, ensure that knitting will remain part of our heritage for years to come.

BOOK No. 172 · PRICE 10 CENTS

Knit for DEFENSE

Chadwick's
RED ♥ HEART

V-NECK PULLOVER
DIRECTIONS PAGE 18 No. S-100

When Knitting Was a Manly Art

By Clinton W. Trowbridge

Clinton W. Trowbridge learned to knit in boarding school as a young boy during World War II. Surrounded by classmates and teachers, all knitting one square after another and tossing them into a bin before casting on again, it never crossed his mind to shun knitting as an activity for girls as school boys would today. He and his classmates were contributing to the war effort and that was a great source of pride. They were part of history.

In addition to "When Knitting Was a Manly Art," first published in the December 5, 1997, edition of the Christian Science Monitor, Trowbridge's work has appeared in Harper's, WoodenBoat, and Reader's Digest. He had also written a number of books, including Grotties Don't Kiss: A Prep School Memoir, published by Vineyard Press in 2002.

Today one seldom sees anyone knitting. Grandmotherly types, likely suspects, pull newspapers or magazines out of their handbags rather than skeins of wool while waiting for trains or buses. And headsets abound among younger women. The only person I know who knits in public is a man, and though he seems oblivious to criticism, his friends tend to make excuses for what is generally perceived as odd or inappropriate behavior.

When I was at boarding school during World War II, however, everyone knitted, including the headmaster, the teachers, and the whole football team. We knitted nine-inch squares, which somebody else sewed together to make blankets and scarves for British soldiers. "Knitting for Britain," it was called. The wooden needles were large and clumsy, not really fit for much else. It was a knit-two, purl-two, mind-less sort of occupation, like mucking out a barn or shoveling snow. But it was wartime, so we all did extra things.

There was a picture hanging up in the school library of the football fields grown up in wheat during World War I. We were not issued rifles or taught to shoot and march in formation as our fathers had been. Pearl Harbor was still a few months away, and we weren't geared up to do anything much yet.

A few boys became obsessed and knit enormous, lumpy, twelve-foot scarves for themselves. But most of us were satisfied to turn out a square or two at a time and throw it in the knitting bin. I don't know who supplied all the wool.

I didn't really think of what we were doing as knitting. It seemed so unskilled compared with what "Aunt" Margaret, my grandfather's second wife, did. A snappily turned-

Knit for Defense

In 1941, Chadwick's Red Heart Wools published this stars-and-stripes emblazoned pattern-booklet for knitters who wanted to create useful garments for American servicemen.

out divorcee just my mother's age, she was the knitter in the family, famous for being able to turn the heel of a sock while at the movies. She knitted argyles with her own patterns on them for the males of the family. She never made just a plain pair of socks, all one color. If she used one color, there would be cables spiraling up the sides, like beans around a pole, or elaborate ribs, or some other design.

Most of her socks were composed of several colors: Gray-and-yellow checks on a field of black is a pattern she made for me. Some had pictures on them: sailboats, top hats, a glass with a straw and a cherry in it. When you put on these socks, you knew you had something special and you were careful to keep them straight. So they wouldn't bag, you wore tight elastic garters, which dug into your calves.

By spring 1942, we not only had work squads—I was on outdoor maintenance, which was a lot better than being on the coal squad—but we were also waiting on tables and feeding the steaming, stinky dishwasher in the kitchen. Gas, sugar, meat, and all sorts of other things were rationed. Getting back and forth from home in Philadelphia to school outside of Boston was twice as hard because of all the sailors and soldiers traveling on the trains.

The next year was even worse. There were mock air raids, which were quite realistic and taken very seriously because there was a large Army base nearby. We spotted planes from the roof of the school (it was always exciting to be on a roof) and telephoned in their identities and approximate positions. With U-boats being sighted off the East Coast, the idea of German airplanes bombing the school seemed only slightly absurd.

And then there were all the graduates, masters, and even some seniors, returning to the campus on leave, heroic in their uniforms. How we envied the knife-edge creases in their trousers, the brilliant shines on their cordovans, and the epaulets on their squared shoulders. War meant driving a car fast across the football field, or

Boys Knitting for the Boys

Bill Dickman, Jack Rosen, Melvin Sinykin, Leonard Strouse, and Arvin Zaikaner, students at Groveland School in Saint Paul, Minnesota, were but a handful of the young American boys and girls who knit for the war effort in the early 1940s. (Photograph by St. Paul Dispatch-Pioneer Press, courtesy of the Minnesota Historical Society)

getting up in the middle of the night and marching down into the cellar in your pajamas, bathrobe, and slippers, holding your breath there in the dark, and listening for the ominous purr of planes.

"Knitting for Britain" became quite competitive. Who could knit the fastest, or make the longest scarf, or make the most noise with his needles? A good many of us took up knitting seriously and made socks, sweaters, and woolen hats. We would knit in bed after lights out and, some of us, even more surreptitiously, in chapel. Finally, the headmaster had to take steps to limit the activity.

"Knitting for Britain" was something of an escape from more serious work, I suppose; therapeutic, perhaps, at a time when life was becoming so tangled. But no one ever thought it odd that a school of two-hundred boys should be busily whiling away the hours in such an activity.

And certainly no one ever suggested that it was inappropriate for us to be doing "women's work." That question, in those supposedly unliberated times, never even came up.

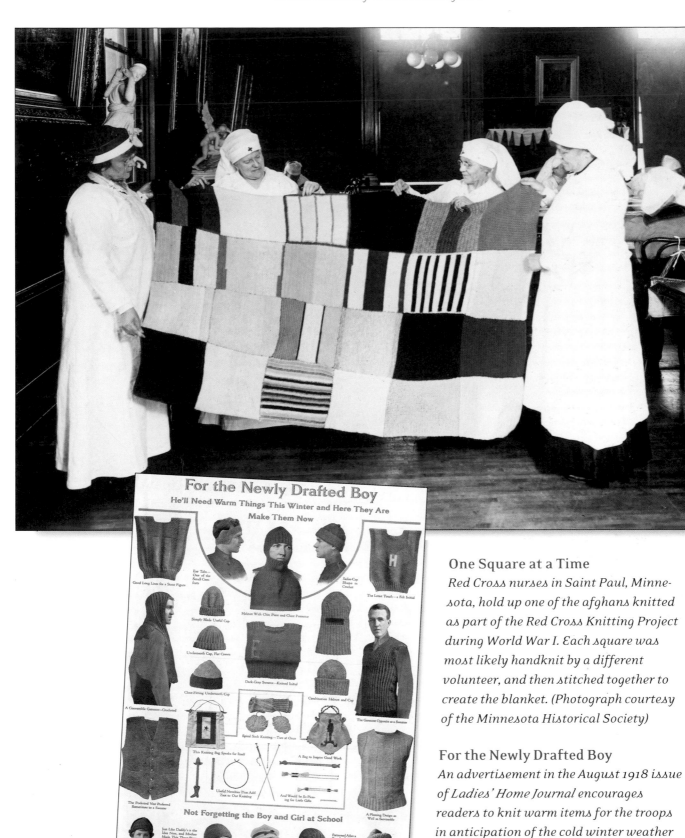

One Square at a Time

Red Cross nurses in Saint Paul, Minnesota, hold up one of the afghans knitted as part of the Red Cross Knitting Project during World War I. Each square was most likely handknit by a different volunteer, and then stitched together to create the blanket. (Photograph courtesy of the Minnesota Historical Society)

For the Newly Drafted Boy

An advertisement in the August 1918 issue of Ladies' Home Journal encourages readers to knit warm items for the troops in anticipation of the cold winter weather to come.

Knitting in Class
Students at Clara Barton School in Minneapolis knit for the Red Cross during the first World War. (Photograph courtesy of the Minneapolis Public Library, Minneapolis Collection)

Knitting Instructions for the Armed Forces
The Canadian Red Cross Society and the Telephone Directory teamed up to offer this pocket-sized booklet of knitting patterns for servicemen and -women, including socks, Hurricane Mitts, and the Quebec Helmet. All items were to be knitted in khaki, the official color of the armed services.

LIFE

HOW TO KNIT

NOVEMBER 24, 1941 **10** CENTS
YEARLY SUBSCRIPTION $4.50

A Lifetime of Knitting

By Denyse Specktor

Knitting artisan Denyse Specktor became a knitter at age five when her mother gave her lessons. She became a second generation professional knitter when her wearable art sold to Beverly Hills Boutiques in the 1980s, the first to Donald J. Pliner's Right Bank Clothing Company. Her book The Knitting Primer, a compendium of knitting information, was published shortly thereafter. Since then, Denyse's media commissions have been seen in films, commercials, music videos, on television, and in gallery exhibits. Her company The Big Yarn Dye-it! provides hand-dyed yarns, hand-painted ribbons, and pattern support to knitters nationwide. Denyse also interviews noteworthy knitters in her column My Knitting Bag, which appears regularly in Knits Magazine.

In her essay "A Lifetime of Knitting," Denyse traces the ways in which knitting has evolved since the days her mother would gather with friends to knit sweaters for the troops during World War II.

As a child I played with my mother's knitting patterns. I begged her to teach me how to produce those beautiful pieces that she seemed to create effortlessly and magically while my brother and I slept. When I turned five, she gave me yarn and my own blue, size eight needles. Many years passed, and I was a teen before I picked up knitting needles again. My mother told me stories of how she and her friends knit as they listened to the radio for news from the front lines, worrying all the while about brothers, cousins, and the boys they used to meet for a soda or a movie who were now overseas. But by this time, the magazines filled with cherub-faced babies and the patterns my mother had from World War II no longer interested me.

In the late 1960s I began to take my knitting seriously. My mother gave generously of her time and continued to enhance my skills. We would go to the yarn store together to buy yarn, needles, and patterns. How limited the selection was then compared to the magnificent bounty we have today. I remember the sound of metal needles clicking away as women knit in the shop. Plastic needles were available, but the metal were the best—so much finer than the steel needles that my mother and her friends had used twenty-five years earlier (I still have some of those needles). The women who knit for the war effort only knitted with dark yarn, never light, because the steel left marks. It was an easy sacrifice—after all, it was for the war effort. Those needles were so thin—I have a sweater made from a cherished tweed yarn ripped from a glorious two-piece dress, originally knit on a size 1, now tripled.

By the mid 1970s my friends began to have babies, and I went to look at the long untouched box of pattern books, graced with the smiling cherubs, but where were they? My mother had lent my patterns to a friend, who had given them to someone else by mistake. A piece of my childhood

Learn How to Knit with *Life* Magazine

The November 24, 1941 issue of Life magazine features a young Peggy Tippett, biting her lip in concentration as she knits a V-neck Army sweater for the troops. A short article inside walks novices through the basic steps to knit the sweater, calling for a million sweaters by Christmas.

was lost. I vowed to replace every single one of those mis-directed magazines. I have located many of the patterns lost, although I haven't replaced them all, and I have discovered many others.

I have books that cover every decade of the twentieth century. Mention an era, name a style, and I'm sure I have just the pattern, which has pleased many costume designers as we searched for the ideal influence for a design for a movie, commercial, or music video.

I thank my mother and her dear friends who started knitting to pass the time during the war years for igniting my passion for knitting. My mother's stories meant nothing to me then, but now they are my heritage—a thread to

the past and the future. The knitting my mother, Lee, did while socializing with friends eventually became her profession. She went on to be a sample knitter of unparalleled skills. From the time she taught me to knit at the age of five through my own development as a hand knitter, my mother encouraged me to dream and to challenge myself. I will always be a student of knitting, but as an educator and author over the past twenty years, I have taught thousands to knit, and I've collected knitting friends along the way. These knitters come and go, but they always inspire me, giving me new ideas for the classes I teach, knitting designs I develop, or the tools I create.

Knitting Class, 1917
Students in a knitting class show off their projects, many of which appear to be standard sweaters for the war effort. (Photograph courtesy of the Minnesota Historical Society)

Knitting for Baby
Baby pattern books from the 1940s and 1950s featured countless layette sets, bonnets, sweaters, booties, and bibs, sized for newborn through the toddler years. Angelic baby faces graced the colorful covers.

Flora Macdonald Steel Knitting Pins
Steel knitting needles were all that was available to knitters during the world wars. The pins were known to leave unsightly marks on the yarn, so knitters resorted to using dark yarn, so the marks wouldn't show.

Passion for Collecting

By Denyse Specktor

While talking to a friend the other day about my vintage knitting collection, I realized I am a collector. Over the past twenty years, I have amassed celluloid, bakelite, bone, wood, and ivory needles; needle gauges; hundreds of knitting and pattern books; and metal and bakelite needle canisters. But my habit doesn't stop at knitting paraphernalia. I began to tell her about the lamps and the linens—the tablecloths, the napkins, and the tea towels. I then realized I hadn't mentioned the buttons, the toys, the aprons.... Stop! I said to myself. Is there a collector's anonymous?

Of all my collections, the knitting is a constant passion. All the others come and go. I don't recall quite when I combined two of my obsessions, knitting and photography. Serendipitously I discovered many wonderful old photos of knitters—everyday people, soldiers in hospitals during World War I, mill workers on their lunch break, young children in school, and old women mingling. The images of knitting royals, political figures, and celebrities are special finds. For hundreds of years, knitters have been depicted enjoying their craft, whether in drawings, early Daguerreotype, or digital photos. We are privileged to have a documented history.

Meanwhile, I've got to run. The mailman should be arriving soon with an ornate yellow bakelite yarn box from the 1950s...

Mr. and Mrs. Roosevelt relax at home.

Clair Trevor, a remarkable actress during the 1930s and 1940s who played a glamorous leading lady opposite the likes of John Wayne and Clark Gable, knits for the Red Cross.

Joan Blondell's big blue eyes, winning smile, and talent won her roles opposite James Cagney in *Sinner's Holiday* (1930), *Public Enemy* (1931), and *Blond Crazy* (1931). Between films, Joan would knit for the war effort.

In between scenes from *My Life with Caroline* (1941), Charles Winninger winds yarn with actress Anna Lee.

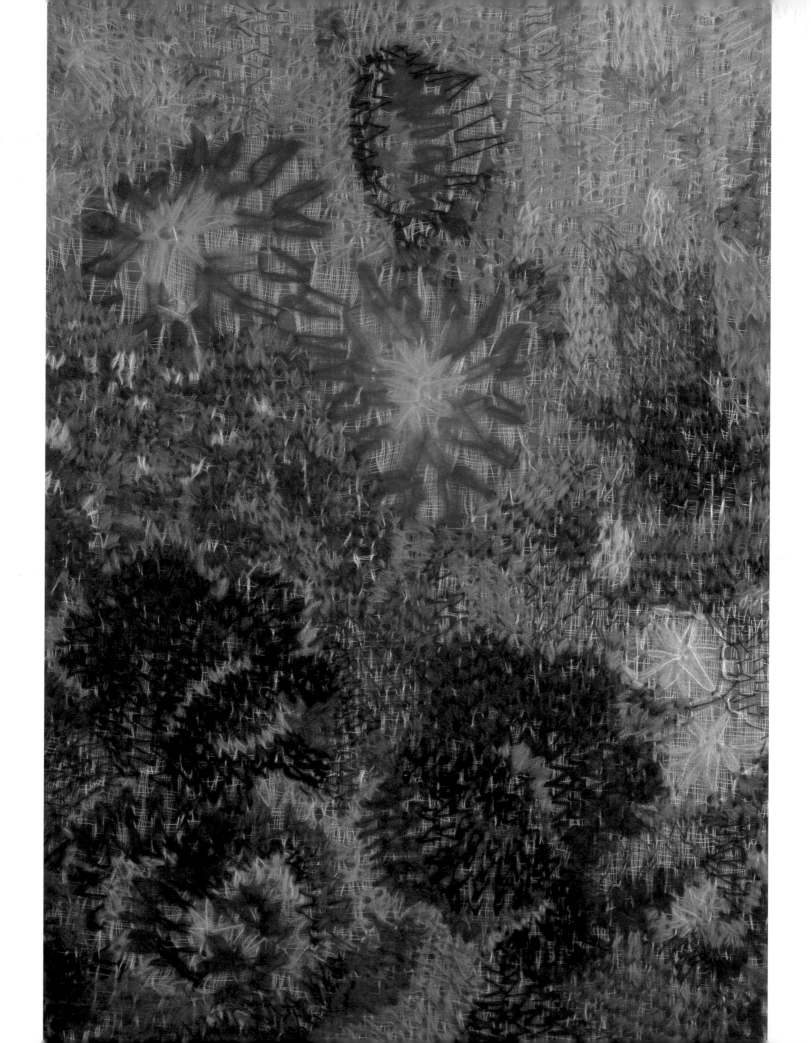

Knitting Camp

By Meg Swansen

Since 1965, when she joined forces with her mother, master knitter Elizabeth Zimmermann, Meg Swansen has been instrumental in teaching people how to knit. Together, Elizabeth and Meg designed knitwear, published books, and produced learn-to-knit videos. Today, Meg continues to design and write in addition to overseeing the everyday operations of Schoolhouse Press, the company Elizabeth started in 1959. Meg is the author of several books about knitting, including A Gathering of Lace and Handknitting with Meg Swansen. She also writes a regular column for Vogue Knitting, and she is a contributor to Knitter's magazine.

Perhaps the most important contribution Meg and Elizabeth have made to the world of knitting has been Knitting Camp. The camp, which takes place in a small town in central Wisconsin, has become much more than a place where people go to learn to knit or pick up new knitting techniques. For those who've attended over the years, the camp has been an eye-opening experience that has changed the way they view knitting, offering abundant ideas and possibilities for the application of the craft. Camp has also become a community. Several knitters return year after year to share ideas, learn from others, and renew friendships. In this essay, Meg reminisces about camps of past years and the many knitters who've brought life and energy to the concept.

We celebrated our thirtieth year of Knitting Camp in the summer of 2003. I've often wished for someone to attend two or three different sessions and try to capture the event in words; preferably someone who does not knit so they can glimpse an overview of the atmosphere and interaction among attendees without being distracted by the dazzling knitted garments and the innovative new techniques under discussion. There have been many magazine and newspaper articles about our Camp but to date, no independent nonknitting writer has stepped forward.

I've never attempted the assignment myself, as being closely involved with every aspect of producing Camp makes objectivity impossible. But on the other hand, I argue with myself, I am in a unique position to have observed this gathering over a span of decades, so here goes. . . .

In the summer of 1974, the University of Wisconsin extension in Shell Lake, Wisconsin invited Elizabeth Zimmermann to conduct a knitting workshop on their campus. Elizabeth's first book, *Knitting Without Tears*, had recently been published and about a dozen knitters attended that initial year. Included in the group were Jean Krebs and Lois Young, and both have not missed a single year since (with the exception of 1989, The Dark Year when there were no Camps).

On the shores of a small jewel of a lake, the Camp was in a lovely location, so late in the summer of the following

Perennial Garden, 1996

Inspired by the blooming flowers in her perennial garden, Debbie New knitted vividly dyed mohair into a large piece of cheesecloth. Although she had originally planned on removing the cheesecloth, she liked the misty quality it lent to the piece, so she left it intact. (Photograph © Brian Céré of Dumont Group Photography, Kitchener, Ont.)

year, my family and I accompanied my parents to Camp. My father, husband, and the kids swam and sailed every day while my mother and I went to knitting class, which by now had grown to about thirty people.

The accommodations were very low key: dorm housing, no air conditioning, classroom desks, etc. It was the attendees who actually adopted the name "Knitting Camp." At that time, one could take the class for continuing education credit, which meant Elizabeth had to assign a project to be graded at the end of the week. I well remember one assignment: Anything That Can Be Worn on the Head Which Incorporates the I-Cord. The twenty-five to thirty knitting brains hatched some amazingly imaginative items! However, because Elizabeth did not have a college diploma, she was deemed unfit to render grades, so another person—who did not knit but did have a diploma—was called in to assess the projects. Amazing.

After about ten summers at Shell Lake, our kids reached the age when the annual trip "Up North" had lost its appeal, so we moved Camp to a nearby town in the center of the state, where it has since remained.

As time wore on, I shifted from being Elizabeth's assistant, to teaching. In 1991 my mother retired and passed the baton to me.

When Knitting Camp began, we offered one week of classes per summer, but as interest in knitting grew and Elizabeth's three subsequent books were published (and her television series were aired on PBS), we started to offer two sessions, then three, and now there are four groups per year.

Campers who returned each year stayed together, forming a snug group and calling themselves Third Timers, or Oft-Timers. At their session, actual teacher-led instruction has been replaced with mini-workshops that campers present to each other on techniques or ideas unearthed during the fifty-one weeks we were apart.

After a few more years another knitting "family" formed (there are almost sixty of them at present), calling themselves 2.75 Timers. At present we offer two separate sessions for First- and Second-Timers.

What makes Camp so extraordinary is, of course, the Campers. We embody a wide range of ages, education levels, life experiences, and occupations. In the early days there were many bold knitters for whom the journey to Knitting Camp was their very first trip away from the safety of husband and home—some of them driving great distances by themselves, with great daring. Now attendees fly to central Wisconsin from all corners of the United States and occasionally from out of the country. A typical Camp may be comprised of women and men who are university professors, stock brokers, lawyers, computer programmers, environmentalists, teachers, yarn shop owners, and young mothers who sometimes bring their new babies with them. Some attendees are new knitters, while others are professional designers and authors who have been encouraged by our knitting-family to submit their designs and manuscripts to magazines and publishers.

Traditionally, knitting was taught in childhood by one's parent or grandparent, but our society has changed a great deal and the "Knitting Grandma" is a cliché that has become relatively rare. Because of this, many young Knitting Campers particularly enjoy the company of the older attendees, and the older ones are pleased to share their experience and expertise with this new generation of knitters.

Deep and long-lasting friendships are formed at Camp and each Camper knows that they are welcomed back, even if they have had a nonproductive knitting year; sometimes real life interferes with our knitting time. Although new acquaintances may have no other contact during the year, they rejoin as old friends once Camp begins again, and conversations continue as if no time had passed. Others who meet for the first time at Camp, maintain contact throughout the year and even travel to meet each other's families. Sisters who live on opposite sides of the country may meet at Camp for their annual reunion and last year we had five sets of mother/daughter knitting teams in one session.

Naturally, there are many people for whom one time at Camp is sufficient. But we suspect that those who return are drawn by our common bond: we are all somewhat obsessed by handknitting and a family atmosphere among attendees is quickly established. We derive enormous pleasure from gathering with the same group, year after year, yet we greet new faces and new ideas with a glad cry.

There is so much more than knitting that passes between us each summer. It is very touching to see the depth of emotion that is generated as we discuss the triumphs and disappointments we have experienced in our knitting and our lives. Many knitters recognize the sturdy connection between one's philosophy of knitting and philosophy of life; it is wonderful to see how frequently and readily they merge into one.

Knitted History
Solveig Hisdal designed the sweater on the left using elements and colors from a woolen bunad bodice from Hallingdal,
Norway. The sweater on the right pulls colors and pattern from a table-braid blanket from the Norwegian city of Eiken.
(Photograph © Solveig Hisdal)

Granny Squares, 1998

When Debbie New set about to create "Granny Squares," a portrait of her grandmother, she wanted the piece to have the same feel as an old sepia photograph. To achieve this, she knit the squares in undyed wool and alpaca, constructing each in the same way one would assemble a log cabin quilt. The blocks are crocheted together and quilted to a backing. (Photograph © Sandy Nicholson Photography)

Triple Exposure, 1994

Using mixed fibers mounted on a polyester backing, Debbie New knitted this farm scene in a variety of colors and textures. A Mennonite farm just outside the town in which Debbie lives provided the model for the buildings outlined in black. Seeing through the buildings gives a sense of the forest that grew on the land before it was cleared for farming and towns. (Photograph © Brian Céré of Dumont Group Photography, Kitchener, Ont.)

Elizabeth Zimmermann, a Tribute

When it began to look as if For the Love of Knitting would actually happen, I spent countless hours poring over knitting books, magazines, and websites in search of possible material to include in the book. As a beginning knitter, this was a dream come true, and I eagerly absorbed everything I read. One name—Elizabeth Zimmermann—appeared again and again in essays, magazine articles, and web blogs. Curious, I picked up copies of Knitting Without Tears and Knitting Around and began to read. It didn't take long for me to understand Elizabeth's appeal. I was immediately drawn to her common-sense approach to knitting. She encouraged knitters to think outside the box rather than to blindly follow patterns. She advised knitters to take accurate measurements, knit a gauge, and calculate stitches per inch to ensure the finished garment will fit. Knitting the Elizabeth way means knitting with a genuine understanding of the garment's construction, while following a pattern without question is akin to memorizing key facts for the sole purpose of passing a test, only to later forget what was "learned."

Given Elizabeth's great contributions to the art of knitting and her still-growing band of devotees, it seemed only fitting to include a piece paying tribute to her in this book. And who better to write the piece than knitters themselves—those who've benefited the most from her clever ideas, words of encouragement, helpful hints, and wonderful sense of humor?

I'm just not convinced Elizabeth Zimmermann got it right, the title of that first book, *Knitting Without Tears*. It should have been *Knitting Til You Laugh So Hard You Cry*. Or *Knitting With Hilarity and Complete Confidence*. Or more accurately, *The Ya-Ya Sisterhood Takes Up Knitting*.

I first met Elizabeth when she attended our Spin-Off Autumn Retreat (SOAR) in 1985 as a mentor. We'd never invited a mentor who wasn't a serious spinner before, and it felt like a bit of a risk. Our guests were passionately, obsessively involved in making yarn. What they did with it seemed, for many, secondary. Would Elizabeth be able to engage them?

The real question turned out to be how to disengage them. How to get them up out of their worshipful circle to, say, have a meal, or go to bed. We're not talking about Blind Followers here, we're talking about Besotted ones.

Imagine this: a comfy large room in a rustic mountain lodge. In the center, in the midst of a motley group of jeans-clad, fleece-toting fiber maniacs, is a serene, grandmotherly woman with luminous eyes, a half-made sweater in her lap. She begins to chat, "spin her yarn," as it were. The story is low-key, personal. It's about knitting, but more than that, it's about *thinking* about knitting. It's about setting aside the rules, challenging the traditional assumptions. The energy builds, and pretty soon it's about sending those old line-by-line patterns up in flames! It's about being free! This is like nothing so much as an old-fashioned tent revival.

Godmother of Knitting
Revered in so many ways for her wit, spirit, and innovative knitting practices, Elizabeth Zimmermann has long been referred to as the Godmother of modern knitting. (Photograph courtesy of Meg Swansen and Schoolhouse Press)

Questions, shrieks of laughter, eurekas, for hours on end. And Elizabeth, still serene but with an impish twinkle in her eye, in the middle of the circle.

The whole weekend was like that, it never let up. Knitting versus purling, circular versus flat. Tension and slant, shape and fit, that magic formula. Odd cast-ons, tricky cast-offs, creative mistakes, just pull on this little piece of yarn and see what happens! She taught us to think like artists, like engineers, like sculptors, like plumbers; she taught us to "unvent," she taught us that knitting could be a slapstick adventure.

And her message wasn't just about knitting (depending on how you define it). For Elizabeth, knitting was a family affair. We came to know the children, the grandchildren, the Gaffer, and somehow we felt part of that cozy group, part of that family for which knitting seemed to be a binding metaphor and a source of endless fun.

That was fifteen years ago, and Elizabeth was beginning to wind down her travel commitments. As years went by and memory failed, she wrote less, taught less, knitted less—yet the joy, humor, bravado, and invention with which she buoyed up going-on three generations of us has somehow prevailed. The legacy is sterling, the memories golden.

—Linda Ligon, Publisher of *Interweave Knits* magazine

* * *

I first heard the name Elizabeth Zimmerman in the summer of 1978. I had come to a seacoast town in Maine to visit friends and share a large sprawling house with three other women, a fellow, and two dogs. One of the women was a knitter and a reader. And I can still remember walking into the kitchen late one evening to find her sitting cross-legged on the floor, working on a sweater unlike any I had ever seen. She was designing it herself using stitches from a book of traditional knitting patterns. She was making it out of a fine natural silk on very small needles. I was impressed. In her pile of knitting books, which spent the summer shifting from one unsticky spot on the kitchen table to another, was a book with the intriguing title *Knitting Without Tears.* At some point during those months, I picked it up and read. And read. *Knitting Without Tears* wasn't a book, it was a revelation. I had just finished a master's degree in linguistics and for years, I had rarely read anything without a pencil in hand, my tool for wrestling something intelligible from weighty tomes on the nature of language and semantics.

Knitting Workshop
Elizabeth provides knitting tips and short cuts on the set of "Elizabeth Zimmermann's Knitting Workshop," a video series that captures the essence of her Knitting Camp gatherings. (Photograph courtesy of Meg Swansen and Schoolhouse Press)

Imagine my pleasure in meeting (through her book) Elizabeth Zimmerman, on discovering that technical writing could be narrative. Here was a manual, a treatise, on knitting that I couldn't put down. I laughed, I guffawed, I clucked. Here was the grandmother, the great aunt, the neighbor to turn to for knitting advice and mentoring. I admired her stories, her respect for knitting and its rich caldron of possibilities, and her irreverence. *Knitting Without Tears* was my passport. She showed me in her welcoming chatter that knitting could be much more than a pattern and yarn, it was, with the right attitude, a mysterious labyrinth of possibilities, worthy of serious and joyful exploration. Here was another country, a country, thanks to Elizabeth Zimmerman, that I'm still exploring.

—Pam Allen, editor of *Interweave Knits* magazine and author of *Knitting for Dummies*

* * *

Half pragmatist, half enthusiast, Elizabeth Zimmermann embraces, embodies the conflicting, complimentary nature of knitting. What would even the simplest of sweaters amount to without both the vision and inspiration to get it started, and the knowledge (of math, or pattern-reading, or practicality) to see it through? Or, conversely, a firm comprehension that all in knitting is eminently possible, combined with the ability to cling to the image of a sweater that lives largely in the mind to see a knitter through potentially long and dull patches? In a voice unique for its delightful bossiness, Zimmermann instructs, goads, chides, and encourages through all knitting's joys and disappointment. Reading her words (particularly those in *Knitting Without Tears*, a personal favorite), one feels foolish for not knitting, and confident that, with her voice in your ear, no project is beyond your ken. She is mentor supreme.

—Lela Nargi, author of *Knitting Lessons: Tales from the Knitting Path*

* * *

Although I did not have the opportunity of meeting Elizabeth Zimmerman in person, I feel I have come to know her indirectly through the knitters with whom she has shared her joy of knitting. So many of them have become wonderfully creative designers in their own right. It was when I began working on the idea of Ouroborus Knitting (knitting garments out of one complete circle) that I first sought out Elizabeth's work for myself. I had heard many references to a design of hers called the Baby Surprise Jacket, and wanted to be sure I was not echoing her work. So I found her pattern and knitted it up. In fact this is one of the very few garments I have ever knit from a pattern. I was delighted with the intriguing idea she had toyed with and was particularly taken with the way she had included extra details, such as a flared back, to make the little garment more wearable. This ingenious and attractive little jacket is quite delightful. I am envious of those who had the opportunity to meet her. I am grateful that I have now had a chance to get to know her daughter, Meg, through correspondence, but even Meg and I have only met face to face for a few minutes. Somehow Elizabeth and Meg have both managed to spread enthusiasm and encouragement to knitters around the world, even those who have never had a chance to meet them.

—Debbie New, author of *Unexpected Knitting*

* * *

Elizabeth Zimmerman and I considered ourselves bookends, she the English woman who spread a passion for knitting in America and me an American spreading the word for colour knitting in England. Her robust humour and forthright language inspired me to be more dynamic in my approach on the lecture circuit. She wrote to me (on read-

Camp in a Book
Schoolhouse Press published Elizabeth Zimmermann's Knitting Workshop in book form in 1981. The book remains very popular with knitters today. (Photograph courtesy of Meg Swansen and Schoolhouse Press)

ing of me in the *New York Times*) commanding I "go out and buy a circular needle, it will change your life!" I did and it has!

—Kaffe Fassett, innovative colorist and author of *Kaffe Fassett's Pattern Library*

* * *

In 1984 a student gave me my first Zimmermann book. It was *Knitter's Almanac*. Small, compact, and green, what a shock and a delight it was. For the first time I entered a knitting world where I could be at home. Elizabeth, explained, digressed to life, returned to knitting, and re-explained. She did not condescend—except to daughters-in-law about wool—and she was a determined and brilliant teacher. I certainly did not think I was interested in "nether garments" or "Christmas fiddle faddle" but I soon learned to read everything. There was never any telling where the most important information would be found. Try page 25 where she begins, "some knitters are hamstrung by superstition."

Hers was the first knitting book that my family found me simultaneously studying and laughing out loud. Naturally I have my original copy, but it is almost a relic, with so many places underlined and the cover no longer attached. Now I have my fall-back copies and all her other books. They are part of my "bedrock list" to recommend to students. Just the appendix in *Knitter's Almanac* is worth its weight in gold.

For my own work Elizabeth was the great encourager, the technical facilitator. We were not making the same things, but what she taught and her attitude are an important part of what has enabled me to become a sculptural knitter. My piece "Portrait of Alzheimers" is dedicated both to my own mother and to Elizabeth, my knitting mother.

I never got to meet Elizabeth Zimmermann, although her daughter Meg Swansen has been generosity herself to me, but I have carried on endless conversations with Elizabeth in my head. Even when I disagreed with her, these talks were a delight. She is deeply imbedded in my work and heart.

—Katharine Cobey, knitter and fiber artist based in Cushing, Maine

* * *

My first encounter with Elizabeth was through a magazine article about her. It was 1980 or 1981 and I was a young and very inexperienced yarn shop owner. The article noted that she taught classes and, being ready to tackle the world of knitting, I wrote to her and invited her to teach for my customers and me.

She came, twice actually, both times with Arnold, and left her remarkable caress on me, my knitting, and the knitting community in my town—an influence that has endured to this day.

She taught about wool, about how percentages will help keep one on track to create a garment that will fit a human figure—no matter what shape. She taught about not being a blind follower; about having the courage to be an independent knitter.

In sharing her knitting philosophy, she also taught me some lessons in life: "Don't wind your yarn too tight": relax and enjoy the process; "It doesn't matter which hand carries the yarn (Continental or 'English')": be open minded; "Use wool" (a renewable resource): be environmentally aware; "If it is too snug, knitting will stretch": be accommodating; "Your state of mind can influence your knitting": your state of mind can influence your life; "Don't blindly follow the 'suggested needle size'": use common sense and be willing to experiment; "Knitting properly practiced soothes the troubled spirit": knitting will help through troubled times.

Elizabeth gave knitters a gift of her spirit and her keen enthusiasm for knitting. She inspired so many of us to forge on, consider what we were hoping to achieve, and to be successful. In thinking about Elizabeth, I looked again at my collection of her books, in all of them she signed "Good knitting," which I believe was a wish for all good things in life.

—Nancy Bush, owner of The Wooly West yarn shop in Salt Lake City and author of *Folk Socks*

* * *

In November 1999, knitters lost our beloved mentor, Elizabeth Zimmermann. No knitter was more encouraging, knowledgeable, or charming than she. I feel very privileged to have attended a number of her workshops and I must share with you a couple of memories.

After I purchased her first book, *Elizabeth Zimmermann's Knitting Workshop*, I was in line with others to have it autographed. When it was my turn, I apologized for "bothering her" (it was the end of the day and she must have been tired) and her response was, "My dear, whoever would have thought I would have written a book?"

Another incident demonstrated her impeccable manners. Most of us know that she only knit with wool, and even then, she preferred only natural colored wool. Well, one year at camp, a knitter brought a very, very colorful and original design knit from genuine acrylic. Believe me, all eyes were on Elizabeth to see how she would react. How did she? She simply clasped her hands together, and said, "Oh my!" The knitter was very satisfied with her response, and I, for one, had a lesson in good manners.

But my very favorite is the year that Cottage Creations published "Bridget and Paddy," and I used the "knitted friends" as my "show and tell" at camp. Her comment, when she saw Paddy, with his white hair and beard, knickers, and Aran sweater was, "that looks just like my Arnold." Enough said, I gave her "her Arnold." At the end of the week she invited me to her home to meet her husband, and for one hour, we had a most delightful visit. I will always treasure the day.

—Carol Anderson, owner of Cottage Creations

* * *

Perhaps it would have been better if the first thing I had done after learning the basics of knitting was to sit down and figure out how to follow a pattern. Instead, I picked up Elizabeth Zimmerman's *Knitting Without Tears*.

After several tearful misstarts, I finally learned to knit in college, making a beautiful garter-stitch scarf out of a copper-colored mohair yarn. With time on my hands during a summer visit home, I found *Knitting Without Tears*, dug some yarn out of my mother's stash and started the Modular Tomten Jacket. I was able to follow the directions,

Knitting on the Go

Fans of Elizabeth may remember a story she tells in her book Knitting Around about knitting on the back of Arnold's motorcycle as they traveled to Madison, Wisconsin. A semi truck kept pace with them for several miles, glancing over now and again to watch Elizabeth work. Upon arriving in Madison, Arnold was sure the truck driver had been looking at his bike. (Photograph courtesy of Meg Swansen and Schoolhouse Press)

even adapting them to a different gauge, and actually made something that looked like the photo. Unfortunately, Mom was a weaver of Art, not of garments, and the yarn produced a cute but torturously itchy sweater christened The Hairshirt.

Still, I felt encouraged by the successful aspects of The Hairshirt. I also felt liberated from knitting leaflets whose incomprehensible code language I found disconcertingly similar to algebra and computer languages. Guided by *Knitting Without Tears*, I went on to make more garments—some of which could even be worn. The tears were long gone (although I still swore); now I was knitting without a pattern.

In *Knitting Without Tears* I learned that a knitter can design and knit in order to fit the size and satisfy the aesthetics of the person who will wear the garment. Here was a knitting philosophy of "just cast on" done to the tune of "My Way."

Then I bought *Elizabeth Zimmerman's Knitter's Almanac.* For each month of the year Elizabeth Zimmerman described her brainchild and then related how she tested and perfected her ideas by "knitting and ripping." Mixed in are related digressions, technical tips, and finally "pithy direc-

tions." Normally, a how-to book would skip the narrative and just give these final directions, but then I don't consider most knitting books a "good read." This book introduced me to the world of conceptual knitting where one can knit, solve knitting problems, or even just think about doing both of those things for the pure joy of it.

Elizabeth Zimmerman led me through the geometric theory pertaining to shawl increases, the mysteries of weaving, the mechanics of cabling, the physics of stitch formation. While I read, I mentally knitted along with the author, tackling tricky Aran patterns, executing perfect weaving, and creating virtual sweaters, mittens, hats, and shawls all while following her conversational stream of observations on life, weather, and wool. As always, she left room for me to choose my own yarn and modify her designs with my own imagination. The results were flawless and not once did I feel compelled to use profane language, but I must admit, my creations were mostly imagined, rarely knitted.

My tattered copy of the *Knitter's Almanac* opens to a stained page (74) that contains a favorite passage of mine:

You may put the private stamp of your individuality on your shawl by doing none of these, but something you have just unvented.

Do you mind the word "unvented"? I like it. Invented sounds rather pompous and conceited. I picture myself as a knitting inventor, in a clean white coat, sitting in a workshop full of tomes of reference, with charts and graphs on the wall.... I have a thoughtful expression behind my rimless glasses and hold a neatly-sharpened pencil. Who knows but that I don't have a bevy of hand-knitters in the backroom, tirelessly toiling at the actual knit and purl of my deathless designs?

Rubbish.

But unvented—ahh! One un-vents something; one unearths it; one digs it up, one runs it down in whatever recesses of the eternal consciousness it has gone to ground. I very much doubt if anything is really new when one works with the prehistoric medium of wool with needles. The products of science and technology may be new, and some of them quite horrid, but knitting? In knitting there are ancient possibilities; the earth is enriched with the dust of millions of knitters who have held wool and needles since the beginning of sheep.

Fair Isle Yoke Sweater

Shown here with a Henley neck, Elizabeth's design for this sweater was ahead of its time. Knitters work the body and arms on circular needles and then join them at the yoke, knitting the yoke as one on a circular needle. The only seams in this design are very short ones under the arms. (Photograph courtesy of Meg Swansen and School-house Press)

Due to my inability to properly follow directions, I suppose almost every article of knitting I have produced contains some "unvention." If I had been introduced to this craft by another route, I might have considered my deviations "mistakes" and not an inspired link in the chain of "ancient possibilities." I might have gotten discouraged by The Hairshirt and a slew of other disasters and given it all up.

The Earth is now enriched with the possibilities Elizabeth Zimmerman opened our knitters' eyes to. My knitting future beckons me; I have plans for designs to improve, skills to master, and projects to complete. It's just too bad she couldn't have helped me master knitting without swearing.

—Sigrid Arnott, knitter and fiber artist, based in Minneapolis, Minnesota

* * *

My first encounter with EZ was on the pages of *Vogue Knitting* in 1988. Using this publication as my sole tool, I, a natural autodidact, had been teaching myself what I thought to be every knitting technique: those necessary to follow the dressmaking-oriented, disciplined instructions for the couture-level garments shown in lush photos. At first glance the "Tomten Jacket" with a cherubic toddler's impossibly plump cheeks encased in the elfish hood of a Tyrolean-style jacket held little interest. Recently everyone I know, including myself, has become part of a new baby boom so now I have a mommy's perspective, but then I just turned the page, thinking "Oh some German broad with homemaker, swaddling stuff."

Five years later I had experimented with designing my own sweaters, acquired knitting machines, tons of books (but, unfortunately not *Knitting Without Tears*) and stockpiled 20 cubic feet of yarn. I was leafing through old *VK*s and paused to read the Tomten article, the one-piece construction catching my eye. I felt guilty for previously dismissing the simple beauty of this garment, not to mention ignoring the wonderful writing—energetic, wise and opinionated, chatty and natural, discussing human shortcomings, peculiarities and practicalities. Hungry for more, I searched through stacks of knitting magazines seeking other EZ articles. I found the Moebius ring, which assured me I was onto something: EZ was not providing mere instructions for a garment but a kind of natural science of proportions and ratios that invited artistic improvisation. I had found a kindred spirit.

I next got my hands on the *Knitter's Almanac*. I found I had independently reached some of the same conclusions— we shared circular knitting as a favorite mode, a problem-solving approach of seeking logic-based, novel maneuvers and constructions, as well as a fondness for natural wools in natural colors. For me, EZ was the ultimate authority and the ultimate liberator. Whenever I doubted the sanity of letting knitting take over my life, EZ's words reassured me the pursuit was worthwhile and pointed the way to unexplored territories. Now, I'm preparing my own knit design collection/knitting tome to be published by Stewart, Tabori & Chang in spring 2005. In the wee hours of the night I leaf through EZ's books, feeling a great responsibility and drawing support.

—Teva Durham, knitwear designer and writer, based in New York City

* * *

In the beginning was the voice, of course. *Knitting Without Tears* was the first book I ever read that talked *about* knitting. I don't mean gave instructions, or described projects, I mean talked about knitting, as a subject, as a passion, as an activity—well, of course she had the best word: as an obsession. And she had me right from that very first page, and that very first line, "Most people have an obsession; mine is knitting." Here was a clear voice, conveying information and giving instructions, yes (sometimes rather peremptory instructions, at that), but also speaking clearly and in character. I read through the first chapter with fascination, happily following her through her discussion of needles, of ways to cast on. I wasn't about to run out and buy new needles, nor was I looking for specific instructions; I just enjoyed the voice. It conjured up for me the pleasures of working with wool, and also the very particular pleasure of talking and thinking about working with wool. It had not occurred to me before this that patterns and stitch preferences reflected personality and opinions; that the question of why you might enjoy working a particular pattern would be interesting to someone who found knitting interesting and knitted garments beautiful. With Elizabeth Zimmermann's voice, a new conversation had started in my own head, and I was ready to follow her anywhere.

I own her other books as well, and over the years (and it must be close to thirty years ago that I first bought that $12.95 paperback) I have made a number of her sweaters—

or at least sweaters freely based on her designs ("Your sweater should be like your own favorite original recipes—like nobody else's on earth," she wrote). But I still go back to the conversational parts of *Knitting Without Tears*, where I most clearly hear her voice—or at least what I have come to know as her voice, opinionated (once again, she had the best word), encouraging, good-humored, and filled with the delight of someone celebrating her obsession, and evoking her private joys and fascinations. "So there is knit-

Knitting Around
In 1989, Schoolhouse Press collected twelve episodes from the popular "Wool Gathering" video series, starring Elizabeth Zimmermann and Meg Swansen, to create the book Knitting Around. In addition to the patterns, Elizabeth intersperses her "Digressions" throughout the book—reflections on her life and on knitting. (Photograph courtesy of Meg Swansen and Schoolhouse Press)

ting as a time filler," she wrote, discussing her philosophy of knitting. "As a brace for the human spirit it is just as effective." With authority, with a relish that made itself plain on every page, and above all with personality and voice, she opened up the knitting conversation to include mind and heart along with hands, all the while keeping the hands properly busy.

—Perri Klass, knitter and columnist for *Knitter's* magazine

* * *

Elizabeth Zimmermann was funny, feisty, and a fabulous source of freedom to knit what you wanted without having to follow someone else's rules. Her EPS system (EPS is Elizabeth's Percentage System, a set of percentages that allow you to knit a sweater knowing your body circumference and the gauge of the yarn) allowed you to make a sweater that fit, and have fun doing it. She encouraged us to try and sell our designs; as a result, many of my fellow knitting campers are now professional designers.

Her enthusiasm was contagious, and we laughed a lot. She encouraged us to really look at our knitting, which enabled us to find and fix problems on our own. She also was interested in new techniques, and frequently surprised us with mind boggling things she had "unvented."

Many years ago a public radio program asked listeners to send in the titles of books that had changed their lives. Elizabeth's *Knitting Without Tears* would have been my choice.

—Lois S. Young, knitter and camp attendee

* * *

In the 1980s, an overloaded schedule of work and community activity forced me to pass up summer camp knitting with Elizabeth Zimmerman. I had bought the first edition of *Knitting Without Tears*, read it and loved her writing, but I never did knit one of her patterns.

Years later in 2004, my husband and I wandered into a yarn shop in Portland, Oregon. "Now there's a vest you could make me!" my husband announced. Elizabeth's Rib Warmer—in tan, his favorite color—hung on a wall right across from the door. It was the perfect project for all the brown wool Ron loves to spin. It's taken a while for me to get around to it, but I'm delighted to catch up with the spirit of EZ, thanks to my spinning spouse.

—Naomi Dagen Bloom, New York City knitter and contributor to *Knit Lit*

Home Sweet Home

Elizabeth and Arnold pose for a photograph outside their beloved schoolhouse, which became their home and the headquarters for Schoolhouse Press in 1959. The press started out providing pure wool, circular needles, tools, books, and original instructions to knitters. Meg joined Elizabeth in 1965, and the two designed sweaters and wrote books. Schoolhouse Press began to publish its own books in 1981, when Meg's husband, Chris, came aboard. Meg and Chris continue to run the press to this day. (Photograph courtesy of Meg Swansen and Schoolhouse Press)

Norwegian Sweaters

Elizabeth's Norwegian sweater, shown here in both the pullover and cardigan variations, features the drop shoulder inherent in traditional Norwegian designs. (Photograph courtesy of Meg Swansen and Schoolhouse Press)